FENG SHUI
ASTROLOGY
FOR LOVERS

FENG SHUI ASTROLOGY
FOR LOVERS

*How to Improve
Love and Relationships*

GERRY MAGUIRE THOMPSON

FOREWORD MICHIO KUSHI

 A GODSFIELD BOOK

To Herman Aihara, 1920–1998

Library of Congress Cataloging-in-Publication Data Available

10 9 8 7 6 5 4 3 2 1

Published in 1998 by Sterling Publishing Company, Inc.
387 Park Avenue South, New York, N.Y. 10016

© 1998 GODSFIELD PRESS
Text © 1998 Gerry Maguire Thompson

Picture research by Vanessa Fletcher

Illustrations by Micheala Bloomfield and Amanda Cameron

Distributed in Canada by Sterling Publishing
c/o Canadian Manda Group, One Atlantic Avenue,
Suite 105, Toronto, Ontario, Canada M6K 3E7
Distributed in Australia by Capricorn Link (Australia) Pty Ltd
P O. Box 6651, Baulkham Hills, Business Centre, NSW 2153, Australia

Printed and bound in Hong Kong

ISBN 0-8069-7060-X

CONTENTS

ACKNOWLEDGEMENTS

This book is dedicated to Herman Aihara, my respected teacher of Oriental philosophy and the art of living in tune with the energies of the cosmos. Sadly, Herman died within days of my finishing it. Herman encountered me at a summer camp in the Rockies in 1983, and immediately asked me to work for him as editor of the books of George Osawa, the founder of Macrobiotics. On the day that I flew to the west coast to take up the job we discovered that the three of us — Aihara, Osawa, and I — all shared exactly the same birthdate and the same Feng Shui Astrology.

Equally important in inspiring the book is Michio Kushi, who was the first person, I believe, to teach this form of astrology to Westerners. I had the good fortune to study with Mr Kushi and then to be apprenticed to him during his private consultations during 1981 and 1982.

Other teachers that I would like to acknowledge are Takashi Yoshikawa and William Spear. My thanks are also due to Feng Shui consultant Simon Brown for his support during the writing.

At Godsfield Press, I wish to thank Debbie Thorpe for commissioning the book and helping refine the concept, and Sandy Breakwell for seeing the project through from start to finish. I am also grateful to my agent Susan Mears for placing the book with Godsfield Press.

FOREWORD BY MICHIO KUSHI

I am pleased to introduce this book on personal relationships, one of the most challenging aspects of our lives. The patterns of love, attraction, and compatibility form one of the most fascinating parts of Feng Shui Astrology, also known as Nine Star Ki.

I have known Gerry personally since 1981 when he studied with me in Boston, Massachusetts, and assisted in macrobiotic dietary consultations.

Gerry has a distinct ability to explain ancient Oriental concepts, which are subtle and complex, in a simple and highly accessible manner that is ideally suited to the modern mind. Recovery of the Traditional teachings of the past, as well as development of new planetary approaches, are keys to creating a world of enduring health, happiness and peace.

Michio Kushi,
Becket, Massachusetts, June 1998

INTRODUCTION

FENG SHUI ASTROLOGY is indeed an extraordinary oracle. I first discovered it as an architect in London during the 1970s. This was a boom time. There were jobs galore to choose from, salaries went up regularly every three months and it was a great time for thrusting, young, up-and-coming professionals like myself. I owned a house in London and a pair of cottages in Norfolk; I worked a three-day week and after regularly putting money away for a rainy day, I still wondered what to do with the extra cash.

But I wasn't happy. Indeed, I was deeply depressed. Yet I didn't realize anything was wrong. However, some part of my deep subconscious did and was casting around for solutions. It was through architecture, in fact, that the answers began to come. For it was through architecture that I had come across Feng Shui, which was still little-known in the West. This was my first taste of the Oriental sciences of the subtle energies of the universe and how they affect us.

So it was that, after one of those life-altering journeys along the hippie trail across Asia and into the Himalayas, I surprised myself by returning home, giving up my job, and passing through that doorway marked "Oriental energies," in

ABOVE: The character for Natural Law portrays the ox – a symbol of strength and survival.

search of my true self. At the age of thirty, this was in all ways a real departure for me – after a lifetime of purely cerebral decision-making, here I was taking a totally instinctive step. I had the gut

ABOVE: Feng Shui Astrology has been studied and practiced for centuries in the Far East.

feeling that by taking the first step in this direction, I would become the person I really needed to be – and that I would become happy. This was how I fell into the wonderful world of shiatsu, acupuncture meridians, Buddhism, holistic health – and Feng Shui Astrology. I travelled to Boston, Massachusetts, then a hot-bed of such studies, and the following day got an editorial job on the prestigious *East West Journal*. Leaving

LEFT: Scribes from the Orient understood the effect on the individual of universal energies, as well as their potential benefits.

behind the regular commercial world, I embarked on a self-made career of following my true passions in life – and making a living from them. This has been my direction ever since.

This book, then, is all about working with the energies of the universe as they particularly affect you, a truly unique individual – not ignoring them, not working against them, but harmonizing with

them. This is the way to make the most of life's opportunities to achieve good fortune, success, and happiness; and to fulfill the potential of one's relationships.

LEFT: *In ancient China, Feng Shui was revered as the the art of emperors – and only emperors.*

BELOW: *An increasing number of people from the West are now becoming interested in Eastern spiritual practices, such as Buddhism.*

FENG SHUI ASTROLOGY

TODAY FENG SHUI is all the rage. Once, in Ancient China, it was a secret body of knowledge that only emperors and their hand-picked consultants were allowed to study or put into practice, upon pain of death. Nowadays, there seems to be a practitioner on every street corner and featured in every newspaper and magazine; perhaps we'll soon find their notices pinned up with the others in public telephone booths!

But Feng Shui Astrology is another matter altogether. Although it has been practiced as long, or longer, it's still hardly known in modern Western society. In the Orient, however, it has been used as a primary oracle for human beings by vast numbers of people in China and Japan, and other countries under their cultural influence, for a very long time. Indeed, it bears marked similarities to the most ancient astrological systems of a number of other early civilizations. Sages consider it to be one of the few remaining vestiges of a world-wide civilization which was destroyed by epic disasters such as those which wiped out Atlantis and the continent of Mu.

ABOVE: Yin and Yang balance the energies of the universe.

RIGHT: Feng Shui was originally the closely guarded secret of the emperor and his advisers.

Actually, Feng Shui Astrology is simply an application of the same principles that later created Feng Shui. However, its aim is to understand the influence of the subtle energies of time, rather than those of space – the direct influence on people,

ABOVE: Feng Shui Astrology gives an insight into the subtle energies of time and its passing.

rather than through the effects of buildings and external landscape. Where Western zodiac astrology measures the influences associated with the celestial bodies and their movements, Feng Shui Astrology gauges the broader interacting energies of heaven and earth, the cosmic energies shaping the universe. It is the ultimate holistic view of life, rooted in the ancient Chinese concepts of Yin and Yang, Chi or Ki, and the Five Elements that are the basis of all traditional Oriental disciplines – from acupuncture to Zen and from Aikido to flower arranging. Feng Shui Astrology is also distinguished from the astrological system of the twelve animals, which particularly express the influences of earth alone. The Chinese have always been pragmatic and the Feng Shui astrological system has evolved as a very practical, down-to-earth business. Although it provides extraordinarily profound and diverse information about people and relationships, it is far more simple to grasp and put into practice than most other systems.

Interestingly, uncannily similar number-based astrological systems evolved independently in other parts of the world, including India and Tibet, before they were visited by the Chinese. Similarities can also be found amongst the ancient civilizations of the Americas. In more recent times, Feng Shui Astrology has also spread from mainland China to many other

ABOVE: Feng Shui Astrology is distinct from the more familiar twelve-animal Chinese astrology system.

Chinese-influenced countries in southeast Asia, especially Japan. More recently still, it has experienced a phenomenal resurgence of interest, alongside Feng Shui, in commercial situations and burgeoning new economies like Hong Kong. The combination of pragmatic and commercial emphasis on the historical interpretation of Oriental astrology has led to a strong interpretative emphasis on words like "lucky," "unlucky," "danger," "good fortune," and "wealth." But this reflects a shift of emphasis away from the original and far more discriminating Oriental usage, such as is found in the *I Ching*; and that is what we will focus on in these pages.

BELOW: The economic advantages gained from an understanding of Feng Shui Astrology are well-known in the Far East.

WHAT YOU CAN GET FROM THIS BOOK

UNDERSTANDING relationships is probably the most powerful and fascinating aspect of the application of Feng Shui Astrology, and that is what this book focuses on. Reading the book will give you a whole new understanding of the forces and energies at work in each and every one of your intimate relationships – whether involving love,  romance, sex, or partnership – past, present, or future. Whether you are after calm stability or sexual adventure, it will help you to understand better your own self and your ability to relate; to understand partners better; to choose more suitable potential lovers; and to get existing relationships to work better, by understanding their dynamics and taking the appropriate steps, spelled out in these pages. You'll get a great deal of information as you go along; and once you've assimilated the material and practiced a bit, you'll be able to use the system yourself. You won't have to go to an astrologer for future readings – the book tells you how to work everything out for yourself, from start to finish, in simple step-by-step stages.

RIGHT: *A fortune teller in the temple (18th-century China). This practice is still a normal part of life today in China and Japan.*

HOW TO MAKE THE BEST USE OF THE BOOK

THE FIRST STAGE is to take a little time to understand the basics of how Feng Shui Astrology works, for it is very different from other astrological systems that you may have encountered. You will also find it an extremely fascinating and captivating system. This is covered in chapter one.

Now you're ready to start finding things out – first of all about yourself. So chapter two shows what Feng Shui Astrology can tell you about your own personal make-up, with particular emphasis on love, romance, and relationship. After that, the next step is to be able to apply the same analysis to any other person with whom you are now, or might in the future be, in a relationship – whether you've lived with them for forty years, or are thinking of going on a first date with them this weekend. This is covered in chapter three.

Chapter four addresses the thorny issue of compatibility and potential for a good relationship, and makes it all very manageable. It shows you how to combine the astrological information about yourself and about the other person, and how to interpret the results as practical indicators. Examples of how it works are provided. After that, you will want to know how to make the best of the combination of astrological types you have in the relationship in question – and that is what chapter five tells you. Let's be realistic – you also need to know how to improve areas where your relationship is less than ideal. No problem!

After that, you may wish to understand the changing dynamics of your relationships over the

ABOVE: Using Feng Shui Astrology, you can discover if physical attraction is likely to endure into a lasting relationship.

course of time. This might include looking back over the past, looking forward into the future, or choosing auspicious timing for any relationship moves you may have in mind. You'll probably begin to realize you've had recurring cycles of experience; now you'll begin to understand why, and find out what to do about them. This is covered in chapter six.

Finally, chapter seven gives hints and pointers for putting all this information into practice. It also provides a brief run-down on how to apply all these principles and methods to other close relationships in your life, such as in your family or at work.

CHAPTER ONE

How Feng Shui Astrology Works

THERE IS A VERY OLD CHINESE *legend that tells how the primary concept of Feng Shui Astrology was first discovered. It is set in the time of the very earliest civilizations in China, which were set along the banks of the Great Yellow River. These habitations were being repeatedly wiped out by major floods when the river burst its banks, over many successive generations. Then, around 2,000 BC, along came a thoughtful and contemplative man by the name of Fu Hsi, who had the idea of constructing earthworks to contain the flooding river between its banks. The idea worked and Fu Hsi became emperor.*

Whilst sitting in silent meditation on the banks of the river one day, Fu Hsi noticed a turtle coming out of the water to lie on the bank. In those times, turtles were considered sacred creatures and bearers of omens, so he paid particular attention. He noticed a very particular and unusual pattern of markings on the turtle's back – a collection of eight hieroglyphics known as trigrams, arranged in a circle with another in the middle. The emperor imprinted this pattern of marks on his mind and, on returning home, ordered the most eminent sages in the land to interpret the oracle. Thus, it is said, began the body of knowledge about the workings of

ABOVE: *The Shaman would seek guidance from the omens by interpreting the cracks in a turtle shell.*

the cosmic energies, upon which Feng Shui Astrology is founded.

This legend is most likely a mythological rendering of history surrounding the earliest Shamanic practices of divination, which were indeed based upon the use of the turtle shell. A question to which an omen or guidance was needed would be ritually put to the Shaman, who would then apply heat to the inner surface of one of the turtle shell's indentations. This would cause cracks to appear on the outside surface of that sector and these would be interpreted by the Shaman as an indicator of the omens. Over a period of time, patterns of cracks which proved consistently reliable

ABOVE: *Fu Hsi, the legendary first emperor of China, drew inspiration from the markings on a sacred turtle's shell.*

would be formally inscribed and made permanent upon the outer surface of the shell. This shell became an oracle that could be consulted in its own right. All this took place at the time of a purely oral tradition, before true writing was invented. Thus the earliest written records of astrological prediction for the rulers of those times have also been found on turtle shell relics. It is from those earliest simple ideograms that the written characters of the Chinese language evolved.

THE MAGIC SQUARE

THE EIGHT TRIGRAMS of the turtle legend eventually became the basis for perhaps the greatest classic of oriental wisdom, the *I Ching*, or *Book of Changes*. In that book, the trigrams are expanded into a method of interpreting all phenomena and thus obtaining guidance on the most auspicious action to take, or how to interpret events. The classic arrangement of these trigrams – the key to everything in Feng Shui Astrology – is known as the Lo Shu map, or "Magic Square."

So the Magic Square, a seemingly simple arrangement of nine numerical characters, is the heart of this matter. We will now discover all about it. It seems incredible that such a simplistic device can form the basis of a powerful and versatile system of divination. But it is true.

Once you have grasped the basics of how this square works, you will be able to apply it to your life at many different levels.

BELOW: The ancient spiritual belief in the "oneness" of all things still survives today in Eastern religions.

ABOVE AND BELOW: *Life-giving Yang energies radiate down to earth from the sun and all other planets in the universe.*

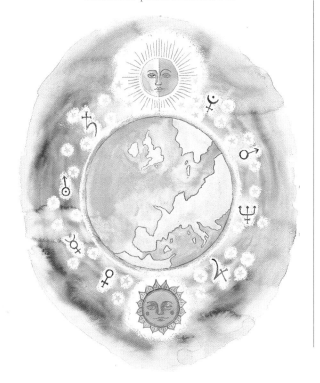

Yin

Yang

ABOVE: *Yin and Yang are interdependent and cannot exist in isolation. Their opposing, balancing powers influence all aspects of life.*

Most spiritual traditions acknowledge the primary importance of the formative forces or energies that activate all life, known as Ki in Japan, Prana in India, and Chi or Qi in China. Astrology is the study of the patterns of change in these energies over time. Basically, the square is a kind of shorthand formula which summarizes the nature of the interaction of these influential energies of heaven and earth, and thus gains insight into the nature of any phenomenon. The phenomenon whose nature and behavior we are most interested in discovering, of course, is ourselves and our interaction with each other – our relationships.

All ancient peoples developed a spiritual sense of the cosmic influences acting on humanity, recognizing the dimension to human existence that transcends the mundane. Shamanism, the earliest of religions, acknowledged this interconnectedness of all things – including human beings – dominated by the interplay of the two greatest forces of all: the energies of the heavens and of

ABOVE: *The continuous cycle of Yin and Yang energies has no beginning or end.*

earth. This view still survives, for instance, in Native American cosmology, as the primary respect for Father Heaven and Mother Earth, who are seen as the originators of all things. This world view evolved, too, in Ancient China, where it was named differently – as the all-embracing interaction of Yin and Yang that similarly produces and characterizes all of life. In the view of Oriental astrologies, then, all life on earth is profoundly affected by these two influences. One is the heavenly Yang energies. These are exemplified by the life-giving radiation that showers down toward our planet from the sun, from other stars, constellations, and galaxies, away

ABOVE: *Fruit ripens in the Earth stage of the seasonal cycle, as Yin gives way to Yang and natural energies start to settle inward.*

to infinity – and most obviously embodied in the force of gravity. The other is the set of opposing and balancing Yin energies that originate in the

central core of the earth and expand outward, physically demonstrated by the capability of trees and plants to grow upward. These two energy fields mix powerfully in all phenomena, notably at the surface of the earth where we live. And the universal law of Yin and Yang acknowledges that these forces always mingle – nothing is only Yin or only Yang – and that their combination in any form is always in a constant but dynamic state of opposition and balance. So all forms of life, whatever form they take, possess a subtle interplay

LEFT: *In an industrialized society it is easy to lose sight of our connection with the natural world.*

THE LO SHU MAP

Tuning your energies to those of the Lo Shu map, or magic square, will take you to the heart of Feng Shui Astrology.

✳ It is the basis for this powerful and versatile system of divination.

✳ It is the key to the energies of the universe.

✳ It is a shorthand formula which follows the movement of the flowing energies around us and how we interact with them.

✳ Grasp the basics of how it works and apply it to your life at many different levels.

✳ In the practice of Feng Shui you will carry out a long tradition of Shamanism that will activate your Chi.

of these influences, which changes from year to year, from season to season, even from moment to moment.

Modern humanity has long tended to forget this subtle interconnectedness of all things and its fundamental significance to our lives. But currently we are perhaps beginning to remember – and even realize that we may need to pay more attention to the earth's oneness if we are to survive as a species. "Touch a leaf," modern quantum physicists are telling us, "and you disturb a star."

THE FIVE ELEMENTS

THE ORIENTAL system of Five Elements is another seemingly simple yet extraordinarily profound method of gaining insight into the workings of life, which evolved from the concept of Yin and Yang. It thus carries us one step further toward the core of Feng Shui Astrology. The Five Element system has been used for thousands of years as the basis of every kind of classical Chinese discipline, from health and medicine to the art of waging war. It also, of course, has its counterpart in the four- and five-element systems that have evolved in just about every other culture that has existed on earth.

The Five Element system goes beyond the acknowledgement of Yin and Yang. It recognizes that everything alive is in a state of changing interplay of Yin and Yang energies in repeating cycles – ascending and descending, expansion and contraction, heat and cold, light and dark, and so on. It also recognizes that there are distinct and consistent stages within these cycles, which can be applied universally – such as in the cycles of day and night, winter and summer, birth and death. Five archetypal stages are identified in this transformation of energies from one extreme to another. These stages have acquired elemental names, but these

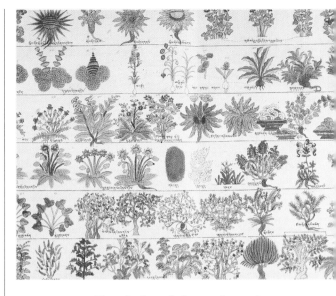

ABOVE: *The cycle of growth, decay, and renewal in plants is one instance of the Five Element cycle.*

terms should be taken more symbolically than literally if the system is to be properly understood. Let us look, then, at these five crucial "elements." Examples from the world of nature and the life of plants are traditionally used to illustrate them.

The cycle of progress through these five stages is continuous and always repeating, without beginning or end, so there is no real starting point. But we can think of it as a circle with a different dominant force at each side and intercept it at the point of changeover between these two types of energy – from the predominantly Yang or downward-moving side of the cycle to the more Yin or upward-moving sector.

RIGHT: *Chinese medicine is concerned with balancing the body's energy so that it flows smoothly through the cycle.*

THE FIVE ELEMENT CYCLE

The Five Element cycle is often described in terms of a natural process of creation. Thus Wood produces Fire, which settles down into Earth. Earth in turn solidifies to Metal, which then relaxes once more into the fluidity of Water. Water then nourishes the growth of Wood, renewing the cycle.

ABOVE: *The creative cycle of the Five Elements.*

WATER

The point of transition is known as the WATER element stage. Yang energy has diminished almost to nothing and Yin energy is yet to begin to be felt – it's a kind of floating between states. This stage in the earth's atmosphere is typified by the season of midwinter, when snow lies deep on the ground. However, the growth potential for spring is already being made below ground, where the dormant roots hold life-force; and soon there is steady

WOOD

movement toward the melting of the snows.

So time passes and we come to the stage known as WOOD.

This is typified by the irrepressible energy of the seedlings germinating, of bulbs pushing up their green spikes, the sap rising in the branches, and the bursting forth of flower buds in a frenzy of sudden and rapid growth.

But this, too, is a passing phase, and as

FIRE

summer approaches, the steady and persistent energy of spring eases. Now we are in the stage of FIRE, where the sun is hotter and the plant world blossoms into flower. There is a quality of peaking of the upward and outward energy, but even as it peaks it begins to diminish. So now that energy comes in more short-lived bursts that suddenly dissipate,

ABOVE: *Spring might be called the beginning of the Yin part of the seasonal cycle, bursting with energy.*

ABOVE: *As outward Yin energy peaks we have the splendor of high summer.*

just like the individual flames of a fire, which shoot up and are immediately gone. Thus the petals fall after a short show of splendor.

Now we pass into the second major phase of the overall cycle. Yin is giving way to Yang and the energies in the natural world begin to settle earthward. It is late summer, the time of fruit setting in the plant realm. This is known as the

EARTH

EARTH stage of the transformation sequence – earth in the sense of the soil or ground in which plants are nurtured and grow.

As fall comes, this Yang tendency strengthens and there is a yet stronger gathering of energy inward – it is the time for the plants to set seed, die back, and then gather their energies into the roots before the approach of winter. There is a distinct pervading sense of the

METAL

contraction and compaction of energies. This is called the stage of METAL.

There is an ever-increasing process of freezing and hardening, before we leave Metal and move into Water again, with its incipient melting and floating quality, and so the cycle goes on. Wood, Fire, Earth, Metal, Water, again and again; in nature's wonderfully complex and subtle ongoing flow. It is life's miracle, when no two moments are alike, and yet it has all happened before.

ABOVE: *Fall is when Yin begins to give way to Yang, a time of settling.*

ABOVE: *At the balance point in the cycle there is winter, when forces are being gathered to begin the cycle again.*

THE NINE ASTROLOGICAL NUMBERS

Now we have proceeded from identifying just two kinds of influential energy patterns to distinguishing five universal types – and we are ready to discover the final nine types of influence at the core of Feng Shui Astrology. The recognition of these nine influences has come to us from deeper examination of the five elemental types, symbolized by the archetypal qualities of the numbers 1 to 9. Number 9 represents the highest and most active level of energies, signified by the stage of Fire element; while at the other extreme, the Water stage is the least active and is symbolized by the number 1. Between these two extremes, the number 5 represents the point of balance – the central point in the Earth phase.

But the Earth element has two extra transitional sub-stages. These are represented by the number 2, signifying Earth energy that still contains a component of rising Yin characteristics – more akin to Fire – and number 8, which is Earth energy with a more Yang, inward-gathering quality, which is somewhat akin to Metal. The remaining two elements also contain two sub-types. Number 3 describes Wood energies like those of early spring's most burgeoning phase, while number 4 is assigned to the slightly mellower nature of later spring. Likewise, number 7 represents the more dramatic early fall phase of Metal energy and number 6 has the qualities of the later, most inwardly-gathered energies.

ABOVE: *Water is the least active of the nine Feng Shui influences.*

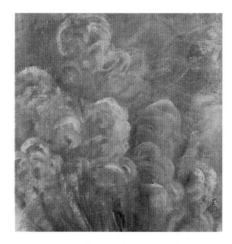

ABOVE: *Fire signifies the highest and most active of the nine influences.*

4 WOOD	**9** FIRE	**2** EARTH
3 WOOD	**5** EARTH	**7** METAL
8 EARTH	**1** WATER	**6** METAL

These characteristics all point to the kinds of personality that are influenced from birth by the respective numbers, and so we shall look more closely at the distinctions between them, and what these mean, in the following chapter.

Finally, these numbers are arranged into the diagrammatic format that expresses their individual qualities and how they relate to one another, thus producing the Magic Square. Now you can discover how to read the Magic Square – and thus find out which of these influences apply to you, and which aspects of your potential for relationship are affected by them.

LEFT: *The position of the number in the Magic Square is the key to the type's personality.*

ABOVE: *The Earth element represents the point of balance in the natural cycle.*

ABOVE: *Wood depicts strong Yin energy.*

CHAPTER TWO

Yourself in Relationships

I N THE LAST CHAPTER, *we saw how the astrological influences acting upon you and your relationships have been discovered and used from time immemorial, and found out the basic qualities of the nine main influences. Now it's time to discover which of these influences applies to you and what they mean. With the insight you have gained into the origins and energy patterns of these characteristics, you will be able to interpret how what follows applies to you as a unique individual.*

So there are nine major astrological influences in this system, summarized in the archetypal qualities of the numbers one to nine. You could compare this with the twelve major influences of Western zodiac astrology. But in Feng Shui Astrology, these nine influences apply to you in three different departments of your being; so your astrological make-up will be expressed as a set of three numbers; for instance 8:4:9, or 4:3:6.

Let's now look at the three fundamental aspects of your nature that these describe, so that you can find out how to work out your set of three numbers from your birth data. You can then obtain guidance on how to interpret the influences in these three different departments of your character.

THE THREE ASPECTS OF PERSONALITY

Your set of three birth numbers sums up the totality of your personality, as influenced by the astrological influences operating at your time of birth and thus making an imprint on your personality. This is rather analogous to the way zodiac astrology takes into account your ascendant sign and the influence of the moon and other planets, as well as your basic sun sign. However, the Feng Shui

ABOVE: *Your Primary Number will have the most important influence on how you relate to others.*

ABOVE: *Working out your own set of three numbers will give you greater insight into your strengths and needs.*

astrological chart is a lot easier to calculate and doesn't require elaborate references to ephemera. So it's a subtle interplay of three influences at once, although in some cases one number may occur twice in the set of three. The three numbers of your birth chart are termed the Primary Number, the Inner Number, and the Outer Number.

Your Primary Number is sometimes also referred to as your "constitutional" or "intrinsic" number. This indicates the influences on your most fundamental personal characteristics as they affect the major life areas – your predominant patterns of personality, emotional life, work abilities, inclinations toward activities and pursuits, ways of expressing your sexuality, social behavior, and so on. This is an expression of the major influences on how you live life in the world. It is also the single most powerful factor in how you are likely to relate to other people, although the other two numbers also have an important part to play in relationships.

The second component of your astrological make-up is your Inner Number, sometimes known as the "character" number. This represents the qualities in you that are usually not so evident in worldly life – your more private, spiritual nature, and your deepest, inner driving force. In many cases, only people who know you well, or who have known you for some time, may be aware of these qualities. Indeed, you may not be terribly well aware of them yourself at present, especially if you haven't done some work in self-discovery.

The third element is your Outer Number, sometimes termed the "energetic" number, which represents how you express yourself, your behavior, and habits – the aspects of your nature that are most outward or "on the surface." These are your more short-term tendencies, your patterns of immediate or reactive behavior – the way you may appear to people who have only just met you, for instance. So your Outer Number represents how you can be when you are not necessarily coming from your most profound being. Nonetheless, it is a vital and necessary part of your individual persona. It too will have a significant effect on your relationships with others and on your own experiences in life.

HOW TO FIND YOUR PRIMARY NUMBER

This number is the most straightforward to work out; it is simply the number of the influence that is prevailing in your year of birth, in the ongoing nine-year cycle. The table gives the number for all the years between 1901 and 2008. Notice that the Oriental year starts about a month later than our Western year, so read off the number for your birth-date accordingly.

9	8	7	6	5	4	3	2	1
FROM FEB 4 1901	FROM FEB 4 1902	FROM FEB 4 1903	FROM FEB 4 1904	FROM FEB 4 1905	FROM FEB 4 1906	FROM FEB 4 1907	FROM FEB 4 1908	FROM FEB 4 1909
FROM FEB 4 1910	FROM FEB 4 1911	FROM FEB 4 1912	FROM FEB 4 1913	FROM FEB 4 1914	FROM FEB 4 1915	FROM FEB 4 1916	FROM FEB 4 1917	FROM FEB 4 1918
FROM FEB 4 1919	FROM FEB 4 1920	FROM FEB 4 1921	FROM FEB 4 1922	FROM FEB 4 1923	FROM FEB 4 1924	FROM FEB 4 1925	FROM FEB 4 1926	FROM FEB 4 1927
FROM FEB 4 1928	FROM FEB 4 1929	FROM FEB 4 1930	FROM FEB 4 1931	FROM FEB 4 1932	FROM FEB 4 1933	FROM FEB 4 1934	FROM FEB 4 1935	FROM FEB 4 1936
FROM FEB 4 1937	FROM FEB 4 1938	FROM FEB 4 1939	FROM FEB 4 1940	FROM FEB 4 1941	FROM FEB 4 1942	FROM FEB 4 1943	FROM FEB 4 1944	FROM FEB 4 1945
FROM FEB 4 1946	FROM FEB 4 1947	FROM FEB 4 1948	FROM FEB 4 1949	FROM FEB 4 1950	FROM FEB 4 1951	FROM FEB 4 1952	FROM FEB 4 1953	FROM FEB 4 1954
FROM FEB 4 1955	FROM FEB 4 1956	FROM FEB 4 1957	FROM FEB 4 1958	FROM FEB 4 1959	FROM FEB 4 1960	FROM FEB 4 1961	FROM FEB 4 1962	FROM FEB 4 1963
FROM FEB 4 1964	FROM FEB 4 1965	FROM FEB 4 1966	FROM FEB 4 1967	FROM FEB 4 1968	FROM FEB 4 1969	FROM FEB 4 1970	FROM FEB 4 1971	FROM FEB 4 1972
FROM FEB 4 1973	FROM FEB 4 1974	FROM FEB 4 1975	FROM FEB 4 1976	FROM FEB 4 1977	FROM FEB 4 1978	FROM FEB 4 1979	FROM FEB 4 1980	FROM FEB 4 1981
FROM FEB 4 1982	FROM FEB 4 1983	FROM FEB 4 1984	FROM FEB 4 1985	FROM FEB 4 1986	FROM FEB 4 1987	FROM FEB 4 1988	FROM FEB 4 1989	FROM FEB 4 1990
FROM FEB 4 1991	FROM FEB 4 1992	FROM FEB 4 1993	FROM FEB 4 1994	FROM FEB 4 1995	FROM FEB 4 1996	FROM FEB 4 1997	FROM FEB 4 1998	FROM FEB 4 1999
FROM FEB 4 2000	FROM FEB 4 2001	FROM FEB 4 2002	FROM FEB 4 2003	FROM FEB 4 2004	FROM FEB 4 2005	FROM FEB 4 2006	FROM FEB 4 2007	FROM FEB 4 2008

I will now explain how to find out each of these numbers from your particular birth details. You will see that all the data set out below are based on the Oriental system of counting time. The actual start and finish dates for all years and months are given, so you just have to check where your precise birth-date falls in relation to them.

LEFT: *The date of our birth dictates our basic type of personality.*

HOW TO FIND YOUR INNER NUMBER

This is the number of the influence in the ongoing nine-month cycle that prevailed during the month of your birth. A simple chart of months and their corresponding numbers is given right. To find your Inner Number, you need to have already worked out your Primary Number. Note the later start date of each month. Just look down the column that contains your Primary Number at the top, and across from the period that contains your birth-date, and you will pinpoint your natal month or Inner Number.

BIRTH-DATE	PRIMARY NUMBER		
	1 OR 4 OR 7	2 OR 5 OR 8	3 OR 6 OR 9
FEBRUARY 4 TO MARCH 5	8	2	5
MARCH 6 TO APRIL 4	7	1	4
APRIL 5 TO MAY 5	6	9	3
MAY 6 TO JUNE 5	5	8	2
JUNE 6 TO JULY 7	4	7	1
JULY 8 TO AUGUST 7	3	6	9
AUGUST 8 TO SEPTEMBER 7	2	5	8
SEPTEMBER 8 TO OCTOBER 8	1	4	7
OCTOBER 9 TO NOVEMBER 7	9	3	6
NOVEMBER 8 TO DECEMBER 7	8	2	5
DECEMBER 8 TO JANUARY 5	7	1	4
JANUARY 6 TO FEBRUARY 3	6	9	3

Finding this number involves a couple of simple steps, which you can easily take if you follow the guidelines below.

When you think about it, your outward nature is related to the interaction of your basic way of being and your more hidden or inward characteristics. Correspondingly, the Outer Number is derived from the inter-relationship of your first two numbers. This is how to discover which number it is.

In chapter one, you discovered the diagram known as the Magic Square. In point of fact, what we looked at then was only the "standard" form of the square, which describes the inter-relationship of the nine influences when they are at their most characteristic stages, at the middle point of every nine-year cycle.

There are actually eight other Magic Square variations, each with a different arrangement of the numbers, which describe the arrangement of the influences in each of the other years in the repeating cycle. So the diagram right shows the nine different squares that express this changing cycle of astrological influences.

Your Outer Number, then, is actually determined by the position that your Primary Number occupies in the particular square that prevailed in your year of birth – in other words, the one that has your Inner Number at the center. To discover it, just follow these simple steps shown right:

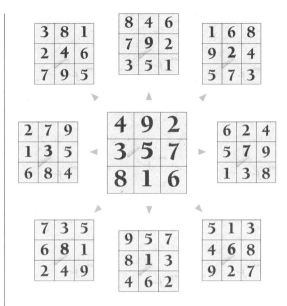

ABOVE: *The Magic Square and its eight variations express the changing cycle of astrological influences*

STEP 1

✳ Find the square with your Inner Number at the center.

STEP 2

✳ Look for the position in this square occupied by your Primary Number, e.g. top-left, corner, middle of the bottom row, etc.

STEP 3

✳ Now look at the central Magic Square – the one that has 5 in its center. Find the number that occupies the position you identified in step 2. This will be your Outer Number. An example of how to work this out is shown opposite.

EXAMPLE OF FINDING YOUR OUTER NUMBER

Let's say you've already discovered that your Primary Number is 8 and your Inner Number is 4. As shown left, you first select the square that has 4 in the middle. You will see that 8 is located in the middle of the top row in this square. Now looking at the "5" square, notice that this corresponding position is occupied by number 9; so 9 is your Outer Number. So your astrological make-up is 8:4:9.

Number 8 occupies this position… ▶

…which is known as the "9" position ▶

3	8	1
2	4	6
7	9	5

SQUARE OF 4

4	9	2
3	5	7
8	1	6

STANDARD SQUARE

ABOVE: *It is essential to determine all three numbers to understand your complete personality.*

CHARACTERISTICS OF THE NINE TYPES

NOW LET'S LOOK at what these numbers indicate about you. The information that follows has been presented with particular emphasis on how it would be interpreted as the Primary Number influence. The same information can be reinterpreted in terms of deeper nature and outward behavior, as signs of your Inner and Outer Number characteristics.

ABOVE: *Pua Kuk holds before his chest the ancient Chinese symbol of Yin and Yang.*

You will see that these patterns of personality traits and tendencies all derive very directly from the nine sub-divisions of the five elements that were demonstrated in the previous chapter. Each of these has also acquired a classical Oriental image drawn from traditional rural and imperial life; this is presented as a title for each of the nine types of influence, together with the corresponding *I Ching* trigram that expresses it.

Precise characteristics given here are generally sample interpretations of the nine broad types of energetic influence. Since each and every individual on the planet is not quite the same as any other, we are all unique and are all open to a different

ABOVE: *Number 1 "Moving Water" types are usually gregarious and have many friends.*

combination of the universal energies around us. These influences have come to be described in poetic or metaphorical terms that enable each person to work out for themselves the precise manifestation that the influence is taking in his or her unique case.

Feng Shui and its Magic Square allow you to do just this.

LEFT: *Like their own element of Water, number 1 types often possess the characteristics of fluidity and determination.*

NUMBER 1 TYPE
MOVING WATER
ELEMENT: WATER

THE NUMBER 1 Water influence is that stage of the Five Element cycle which marks the end of the descending Yang energies and the beginning of the rising Yin flow; so there is a pervasive quality of floating between states. At the same time, there are other, more definite attributes associated with the distinctive qualities of moving water. The common poetic image adopted in the Oriental tradition is that of water that falls as drops on the mountain tops, then forms streams that flow rapidly downhill, merging with others to create a great river, which eventually flows into the mighty ocean.

ABOVE: *The power and unstoppable motion of moving water.*
RIGHT: *The trigram for the number 1 type means "Moving Water."*

Hence, along the way, the element of water displays many powerful attributes – its constant readiness for motion; its ability to sustain long and difficult journeys, its irresistibility in eventually reaching its ultimate destination. It shows its ability to flow round all obstacles, creating its own path through unknown terrain, and slowly wearing down hard rock; its hidden depths when still; its lack of its own form, with adaptability to the shape of any container. People under the influence of this sign will therefore possess corresponding characteristics. Overall, some Water people display more of the adventurous and youthful "mountain stream" qualities, whilst others are more dominated by the "still waters run deep" aspect.

The number 1 type is also associated with that time of winter when the snow lies on the ground, but when preparation for spring is going on unseen amongst the plant bulbs and tree roots. This image implies the potential for inner or spiritual strength that may go unnoticed, but which can reveal itself in demanding circumstances, or when the right time comes in the order of things.

ABOVE: *Some number 1 types show the adventurous, active characteristics of fast-moving water.*

So broad kinds of characteristics emerge from this picture, even if precise aspects vary from person to person.

These people are usually sociable and outgoing, with many acquaintances. They tend to be easygoing or even serene, adaptable and eager to please rather than to cause any trouble. These qualities may sometimes appear as indecisiveness, lack of direction, or being easily swayed. There are hidden emotional depths, or mysteriousness, and it's often difficult for others to tell what's going on in these people's minds. Though generally sociable,

LEFT: *...whilst with others there is an element of mystery, and still waters can run very deep!*

PERSONALITIES

1 types tend to be creative, vigorous, active people, like politicians, actors, or sportspeople. Examples include:

Nelson Mandela ★ Van Morrison
Queen Victoria ★ Eric Clapton
Henry Miller ★ Andy Warhol
Clark Gable ★ Errol Flynn
Charles Darwin

LEFT: *South African leader Nelson Mandela.*

RIGHT: *Actor Clarke Gable.*

they can also enjoy solitude, and are familiar with the world of spirituality and the invisible. They are patient, and worry unnecessarily.

Love can be a weakness. These people have strong sexual desires and enjoy intimacy, and they may not necessarily always enjoy monogamy. Yet

ABOVE: *The number 1 Water element is surrounded by Earth and Metal in its standard position on the Magic Square.*

sex is a very deep and personal matter to them, not to be taken lightly, and they like to consider things well before entering into a sexual relationship. They can be scared about getting hurt and can become insecure and doubting of present relationships if this has happened to them before.

Though they stand on their own two feet, their own success can often depend on the friendship, the partnership, or the beneficial influence of another person.

NUMBER 2 TYPE
THE EARTH
ELEMENT: EARTH

THE CHING TRIGRAM for this influence is called K'un, which means "receptivity," or "bringing to completion." The associated natural image is that of mother earth – accepting energies given from the universe, enabling her to dedicate herself to nourishing and embracing life on the planet; together with all the sustained input of time and hard work that this implies.

People born with this as their primary influence inherit broadly corresponding qualities. They are usually patient and diligent, often thoughtful and reserved, but persistent in the face of difficulty.

ABOVE: *Caring and compassion are the number 2 type keywords.*

RIGHT: *The trigram for the number 2 type means "Field."*

They enjoy helping and nourishing others, even when they find themselves in a leadership capacity. In either gender, there is a strong feminine aspect, although it may not necessarily be revealed in

BELOW: *Feminine "mother earth" qualities – in both genders – symbolize the number 2 type of personality.*

PERSONALITIES

2 types tend to be thoughtful, reserved, caring, persistent in the face of difficulty. Examples include:

Tony Blair ★ Marilyn Monroe
The Dalai Lama ★ David Lean
Allen Ginsberg ★ Indira Gandhi
Alfred Hitchcock ★ George Lucas

RIGHT: *The Dalai Lama has many strong traits of the 2 type.*

LEFT: *Tony Blair, the British Prime Minister, is a born leader who is caring and thoughtful. A typical 2 type.*

ABOVE: *The Earth element in relation to the other eight influences on the standard Magic Square, surrounded by Fire and Metal.*

public. These people are perceptive of other people's character and problems, and are able to make others in their company feel at ease and comfortable.

In relationships, number 2 people can be devoted and attentive to their partner's needs, but may tend to be reticent or overly conciliatory. Even though meticulous, they are stronger on ideals and aspirations than on the practical application of their ideas. They are more inclined to be conservative than unconventional. To them, sex is often a wonderful way to take care of other people, and it is this caring and compassionate touch that often attracts others to them. They want to have another person there to receive all that nourishing from them, rather than being so intensely interested in the sex for its own sake. They should beware of self-sacrifice.

NUMBER 3 TYPE

THUNDER

ELEMENT: WOOD

THIS TYPE EMBODIES the first energies of early spring – the unstoppability of new growth, the sense of rebirth and renewal – the quality of a young tree, whose branches reach up enthusiastically, but whose roots are not yet deep. The *I Ching* trigram describing this type evokes thunder's sudden explosive energy and bursts of lightning that illuminate the sky. Corresponding personal qualities include acute sensitivity, vibrancy, and an urgent sense of quest for life's new experiences.

Indeed, the 3 type person is spontaneously interested in all kinds of different activities and

ABOVE: *Energetic, vibrant, and sensitive describes the number 3 type.*

RIGHT: *The trigram for the number 3 type means "Thunder."*

experiences, in living for pleasure and fun, and in enjoying movement and action. Possessing the spirit of youth, this person tends to be ambitious, humorous, independent, sociable, and idealistic.

BELOW: *Like a growing tree in spring, number 3 types reach out energetically to embrace life's new experiences.*

At the same time, those originating energies also produce someone that can be hasty or rash, unpredictable, not terribly practical, and a rather superficial thinker. Determination is definitely there, but it may not be accompanied by the patience to follow projects through to the end. This person is tempted to move on to the Next Big Thing.

PERSONALITIES

3 types tend to be hasty or rash, ambitious, and social people.

Examples include:

Adolf Hitler ★ Mick Jagger
Robert de Niro ★ Robin Williams
Jimmy Connors

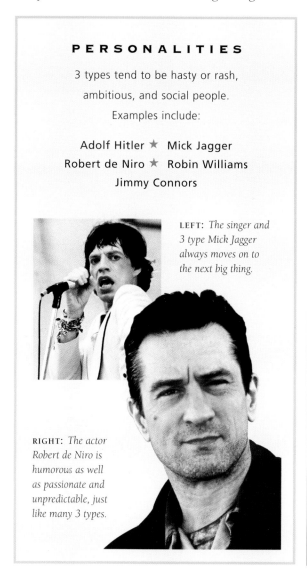

LEFT: *The singer and 3 type Mick Jagger always moves on to the next big thing.*

RIGHT: *The actor Robert de Niro is humorous as well as passionate and unpredictable, just like many 3 types.*

ABOVE: *The number 3 (Thunder) position on the standard Magic Square.*

The sexual drive of number 3 is usually very strong and impulsive, like nature's need to release the pent-up energies of spring, although this can sometimes seem just too strong and be suppressed. If a suitable partner is found, sex with the 3 is usually creative and energetic.

In relationship, 3 is usually positive, open, and honest, but sensitive enough to be easily hurt. He or she is charming and indulgent in sensorial pleasures, falls in love easily, is communicative but too often brutally frank. His or her bursts of passionate energy can be a great asset in a relationship, especially to some types of partner, but to others it can all seem just a bit too much. The 3 type person would be advised to pay attention and listen to the other person – or they may possibly end up alone.

NUMBER 4 TYPE

THE WIND

ELEMENT: WOOD

THIS SECOND TYPE within the element of Wood corresponds to the energies of later spring, when the basic drive of growth and expansion is more dispersed. Even more elementally, this sign is also associated with the wind. Many personal qualities are derived from this. The wind can vary from the gentlest of breezes – indicating qualities of tenderness and affection – to the powerful emotions symbolized by a raging gale. And along the way there can be windlike changeableness in direction, turbulence of feelings, confusion and lack of clarity, or single-mindedness of purpose.

The compassionate and loving aspects of the number 4 type manifest particularly in relationship and social settings, where there is an innate desire

ABOVE: *...or the force of a destroying tornado.*

RIGHT: *The trigram for the number 4 type means "Wind."*

ABOVE: *Wind can be associated with a warm, caring personality...*

to take care of others. Sexually, there is a strong desire for things to be harmonious, romantic, or even sentimental, which can sometimes border on naiveté. They can have very high ideals in these matters and as a result may be let down or hurt. Even so, they might be up for a bit of a fling whilst waiting for the true Ms or Mr Right to come along – the one who matches their inner photofit!

Communication and intuition are usually strong points; 4 is also ready for intimacy, easygoing, and often charismatic, and therefore much appreciated by potential and existing partners. But the capacity for less desirable relationship qualities may need to be addressed: the seeming indecision, acting on impulse or whim, changes of mind, and lack of consistent willpower. Number 4 people can be taken in and give their trust inappropriately, or be

PERSONALITIES

4 types tend to be changeable, turbulent, impulsive, but self-reliant people. Examples include:

Kenneth Branagh ★ Joan Collins
Jimi Hendrix ★ Martin Scorcese
Orson Welles ★ Rudolf Steiner

LEFT: *Jimi Hendrix, the legendary guitarist, at times showed the 4 type's turbulence of feelings.*

RIGHT: *The 4 type's single-mindedness is exemplified in Joan Collins, the actress.*

ABOVE: *Number 4 types are usually good at communicating, but they can also be gullible or too easily influenced.*

ABOVE: *The number 4 (Wind) position on the standard Magic Square, with Wood below and Fire beside it.*

overly influenced by others. They need to develop the capacity for self-assertiveness and self-reliance. But never mind – when things go wrong, they always bounce back from failure in relationships, or anything else, and succeed next time!

NUMBER 5 TYPE

CENTRAL POWER

ELEMENT: EARTH

THIS SIGN IS traditionally associated with the centralized power of the king or emperor, the holder of primal power in the land, who balances opposites and extremes – the great controller who possesses both highly creative and highly destructive capabilities.

As we have seen from the Magic Square, the 5 character stands alone, distinctly central, where all the other numbers connect together and support one another in a circular pattern around it. This is the main clue to all of number 5's distinctive characteristics. This person is perfectly capable of influencing and organizing all the other personalities and is very much used to being at the center of things. Often acting with strength and boldness, he or she can be enormously helpful, supportive and

ABOVE: Hang on tight! Nothing stays on an even keel for long for number 5s, who can expect many ups and downs in their lifetime.

positively influential to others, but can equally be egotistical, manipulative, and inconsiderate. Likewise, this person is destined for extreme and often unexpected experiences in life – big highs, big lows, and equally big turnarounds. Such a person is also very well equipped to deal with all this and more – enduring failures, hardships, and crises that would destroy lesser mortals.

In relationship, the need to maintain a kingly show of strength and emotional self-sufficiency can mean that ordinary needs such as affection are not expressed. Number 5s therefore tend to have few really close,

LEFT: If you are a number 5, you will feel happiest when controlling a situation – as well as the people around you.

intimate friends; but then, many of them are perfectly happy this way. Either way, the 5 will enjoy being a center of attention. But his or her very direct expression of opinions can be tactless and can often cause hurt to any partner who lacks robustness. The avoidance of a middle way, the extremes to which 5s quickly gravitate – highly moral or deeply

PERSONALITIES

5 types tend to be strong, bold, and influential people, but could be egotistical. Examples include:

Mahatma Gandhi
Ludwig van Beethoven ★ **Madonna**

LEFT: *Madonna can be a bold, influential, creative but egotistical 5 type.*

RIGHT: *Hero and leader Gandhi was an example of all that is good in a 5 type.*

immoral, ambitious or lazy, creative or destructive – can also take some dealing with by a lover or spouse. Relationships with 5s may be subject to the same kinds of extremes and ups and downs, by someone who can stand upset and turmoil, and be a beggar as well as a king. Partners of 5 types can have a tough time of it.

Sex is of central importance to them, but again the propensity to all-or-nothing looms large; it probably has to be either a detached physical thing or a deeply committed involvement, with few options in between. If the relationship is the latter, the 5's commitment can be as strong as anyone's and if the roller-coaster experiences are survived, it can become an extremely satisfactory and durable relationship. 5s are notorious for having people come to them rather than the other way round.

NUMBER 6 TYPE

HEAVEN

ELEMENT: METAL

THE NUMBER 6 type represents the time of harvest, with its strong sense of energies gathering inward. The trigram that summarizes this character symbolizes heaven, as the active, creative principle of the universe – evoking personal qualities of order, constancy, perfection, organization, discipline, and completeness. The other side of this coin is that there are also the qualities of rigidity, pride, and inflexible will. It's all very Yang. The number 6 person is inclined to noble attitudes and high ideals, with plenty of inner strength and courage, and preparedness to take risks on matters of principle. The 6 mind is efficient and calculating, persistent and strong-willed, ready to conquer any

ABOVE: *"Heaven" type personalities tend to be perfectionist and high-minded.*

RIGHT: *The trigram for the number 6 type means "Heaven."*

obstacle that may be in their way. 6 types tend to be active, eagerly meeting opportunities head-on rather than waiting for opportunity to come to them. They will battle for what they think is right and tenaciously push their point of view upon others; they feel they know what's best and that is that. They are very much the Yang character.

Sexually, 6s are idealistic, with quite a moral stance. They also tend to insist on everything about the act being exactly, scrupulously proper, which doesn't do a great deal for spontaneous urges and being "in the moment."

The number 6 person is also strong on family values and usually loyal in love and romance. But he or she is often able to dominate the other person, does not like to be the loser or even the subordinate, has difficulty with criticism, and can seem

LEFT: *The number 6 type is idealistic and places great importance on the family, but may tend to dominate.*

emotionally reserved or even somewhat cold. Partners of this person usually do well to let the 6 take the lead (or let them think so, anyway!). He or she can be guilty of using other people to his or her own ends and may have difficulty focussing attention outward, away from the self and toward others. The tendency to stubbornness and lack of

ABOVE: *The position of the strongly Yang number 6 on the standard Magic Square.*

adaptability can also be a factor in relationship situations. The 6 person is therefore advised to allow a little Yin energy into their life – to cultivate a modicum of selflessness, warmth, and consideration for others, practice listening – and let other people have what they want, even when the number 6 knows what would really be better for them! Taking care of this aspect, the influence of 6 can be a very strong and positive influence in any relationship.

PERSONALITIES

6 types tend to be noble in thought and ideal with plenty of inner strength. They are strong-willed and stubborn. Examples include:

Mikhail Gorbachev ★ Richard Nixon

James Dean ★ John Lennon

Sharon Stone

LEFT: *The film star Sharon Stone has been known for her persistence and strong will.*

BELOW: *Ex-Russian leader Mikhail Gorbachev has the noble attitudes of many a 6 type.*

NUMBER 7 TYPE

HARVEST

ELEMENT: METAL

THE IMAGE for this sign is that of celebration of the fruitfulness of fall and material plenty. This generates human qualities of joyfulness, pleasure, entertainment, celebration, and material gain, with a penchant for fashion, dining out, entertaining friends, holding dinner parties – all key concepts in the number 7 person's world view. The trigram for 7 means "The Lake" – symbolizing the qualities of water, whose depth provides nourishment and whose surface offers reflection. This reflective inner aspect and mental sharpness can seem to be in stark contrast to the potentially hedonistic exterior. Commercially oriented Chinese

ABOVE: Fruitfulness and plenty are the 7 type keywords.

RIGHT: The trigram for the 7 type means "The Lake."

astrology, with its emphasis on material prosperity, considers this sign to be the most fortunate of all; but of course this is an artificial and partial view – not the whole story at all.

Number 7 types, then, are competent at managing their business and other affairs – and those of others. They work hard and then enjoy the fruits of their labor with equal dedication. They like spending money, for instance! They diligently pursue happiness and enjoyment with great gusto. They enjoy being well known and well liked.

7s can be very sincere and charming, and sensorially or sexually persuasive. They do want to be loved and are skilled at giving pleasure; however, the aim of the whole thing can often seem to be self-validation. All too often they are resistant to the change that may be needed to make things work – unless, of course, it's the other person that's going to do the changing!

ABOVE: As the symbol of the "Harvest" implies, number 7 types enjoy the bounty of the earth – good food and wine, as well as the company of friends.

PERSONALITIES

7 types tend to be creative, vigorous, active people, like politicians, actors, or sportspeople. Examples:

Prince Charles ★ Francis Ford Coppola
Andrew Lloyd Webber
Michelle Pfeiffer ★ Mike Tyson

LEFT: *The film director Francis Ford Coppola has the 7 quality of being able to organize others and persuade them as to a course of action.*

RIGHT: *The 7 type's creativity is exemplified by Michelle Pfeiffer.*

ABOVE: *The position of the number in the Magic Square is the key to the number 7's personality.*

In relationships, 7s are intuitive and sensitive to the moods of others – which is very valuable – but also able to use this ability in a calculating or self-interested way. They like to be free and unconstrained by another and are cautious about becoming committed to long-term relationships. But they are respectful and good people to confide in. They are generally optimistic, but can be subject to moodiness, oscillating between joyfulness and introspection. Relations with the opposite sex are of fundamental importance to 7s; they experience strong passions and attractions. They should probably choose lovers carefully – with the heart rather than the head – beware of arrogance, and cultivate sensitivity and emotional generosity, in order to benefit their lives in relationships.

NUMBER 8 TYPE

THE MOUNTAIN

ELEMENT: EARTH

OF THE THREE EARTH SIGNS, this is the most Yang and inwardly directed in its formative energetics. The essence of 8 is the mountain that rises above everything else, unmoving and immovable, offering far-reaching views from its peak. This translates into qualities such as firmness, stability, tenacity, and a far-reaching perspective on life; together with corresponding potential weaknesses: stubbornness, pride, haughtiness, and possible loneliness or isolation. They can be resistant to change, immobile in attitude.

Number 8 people have strong powers of concentration and think deeply about things –

ABOVE: *Number 8s may appear unyielding, but can be gentle underneath.*

RIGHT: *The trigram for the number 8 type means "The Mountain."*

indeed, they sometimes think too much – and they have carefully thought-out points of view, which they may be slow to let go of. They gradually learn life skills over time, steadily accumulating learning and lessons from their experiences.

Number 8 relationships can benefit from the virtues of determination, endurance, and strength of mind and will; but this same strong will can often be imposed detrimentally on others. The ego and high self-esteem can often lead the 8 to think of self first. There are strong emotions and desires, but these are not always expressed, or even shown. So

LEFT: *Like their symbol the Mountain, number 8s are steadfast and enduring by nature. Negative traits, however, may include stubbornness and pride.*

8 people often resist advances and can be hard to get to know. Although obstinate outside, however, they are usually more soft, gentle, and yielding underneath. Sometimes jealousy can be an issue. They are generally steady, reliable, trustworthy, and honest in relationships, and able to be faithful and constant in a partnership, in which their inner strength is a very considerable asset.

Number 8s can be very private, in particular with their sexual identity and its outward expression, which can lead to repression. The more the number

RIGHT: *Stephen Spielberg shows the 8 type's epic powers of concentration.*

LEFT: *The civil rights leader Martin Luther King proved a tenacious leader, strong and capable, with a deep regard for life.*

ABOVE: *The position of the number 8 on the Magic Square reflects its deeply Yang quality of inwardly directed energy.*

8 types learn to express themselves confidently the better; but the effort to get to know the 8 type and delve their depths is well worth it. When things do work out right, however, they are capable of finding deep fulfillment and are particularly faithful.

NUMBER 9 TYPE

FIRE

ELEMENT: FIRE

THE NATURE OF this sign is strongly hinted at by the archetypal aspects of the summer sun and of fire itself – its brightness and clarity, its attractive and hypnotic flame, its burning frenzy and the heat that it radiates, its flickering quality and ultimate return to quietness, as each individual flame exhausts itself and dies down.

So number 9 people usually display qualities of brilliance, and love to be a "star"; they are very interested in fame and success, and have a strong interest in matters of beauty and taste. External appearances are very important to them. As they follow their path in life, they shine a light for both themselves and others. Alongside this, they can be

ABOVE: *Others are drawn to the emotionally expressive number 9 types.*
RIGHT: *The trigram for number 9 means "Fire."*

fickle and vain, impatient and inconstant; and underneath their hot, passionate surface there can be a cooler inside.

These people are active, with intense bursts of energy. They make contact with a great number of people, though most of these friendships and relationships are not profound. They like to do many different things, but lack singleness of purpose and perseverance in following through to completion.

In matters of relationship, 9 people are lively, outgoing and sociable, naturally attractive to others, and good at attracting attention to themselves. They are passionate, emotionally expressive, excitable, and affectionate – quick to anger, but quick to calm down again. They are good communicators.

LEFT: *Bright, hot flashes of fire describe the energetic number 9. These people, like their symbol, can flare up suddenly before cooling off again just as rapidly.*

PERSONALITIES

9 types tend to be beauty-lovers with taste, who light the way for others. They can be vain and hard-hearted though social people.
Examples include:

Mother Teresa ★ Saddam Hussein
Walt Disney ★ Liza Minelli
Bill Gates ★ Victor Hugo ★ Eva Peron
Cher ★ Robert Redford

LEFT: *Mother Teresa enlightened many.*

BELOW: *The actor Robert Redford combines fame and success with beauty and taste.*

ABOVE: *Number 9 represents the highest and most active level of energies, signified by the Fire element.*

However, they tend to proceed impulsively, and sometimes without regard for others. They can easily feel trapped and can have difficulty with commitment of any kind.

Sexually, they seem to be able to attract people without even trying. They are happy to accept sex as part of the joy of life in a straightforward way that leaves no room for guilt or anything like that. They are also very romantic. Love is extremely important to them. For better relationships, it can be very good for 9 types to develop self-control and persistence, and also to avoid undue influence from stronger individuals.

The tribulations of any relationship with a 9 type can be easily outshone by their intense energy, feeling, and beauty.

APPLYING THE NINE TYPES TO YOUR CHART

Now it's simply a matter of interpreting the characteristics of the nine types, in terms of the personality categories of your three numbers, representing your primary nature, your inner nature, and your surface nature. This can be demonstrated with an example.

EXAMPLE

Let's take a man whose numbers are 8:4:9. This person has a dominant energy of the 8 "Mountain" type, into which are woven the influence of the two other numbers. He will, for sure, have those qualities of far-sightedness, stability, and tenaciousness in some departments of his life; and there will be the other side of that coin as well – the tendency to stubbornness, the pride and desire for status, the sense of superiority that can lead to isolation. He will also be able to think deeply and concentrate strongly – sometimes too strongly and too deeply.

ABOVE: *The Chinese character for "Long Life."*

LEFT: *The "Mountain" type may be slower than some to learn life's lessons, but will retain the knowledge he gains.*

He will put great energy into building up his life determinedly over time, methodically putting elaborate plans into practice. He's probably one of those late starters, who gets the hang of things later in life, by trial and error, but doesn't forget any of the lessons he's learned, and by midlife he knows how to be happy. His sexuality will primarily stem from this part of his character, which may not make for the most dynamic sexual expressiveness around.

Yet at the same time the far more ephemeral energy of 9 strongly colors this underlying pattern, producing perhaps a habit of sorting quite a lot of things out on a moment-to-moment basis, which can often compromise his monolithic stability, wisdom, and capacity for foresight. So the calm steadiness can give way to superficial and mercurial changes of mind, until at last there is recourse to deeper and better judgement.

There may well also be an irrepressible and optimistic quality in this person's basic motivation and driving force in life, stemming from the four energies, which could also manifest in his approach to spiritual matters and "the meaning of life." This will probably not be visible to casual acquaintances, but those who are closest to him will gradually notice it, from subtle and understated signs rather than blatant self-advertisement. These confidants may well be inspired and uplifted by this positive influence. This person's intuition can also be extremely strong and of great value, if it is trusted, cultivated, and brought to bear on ordinary life. The Wood element energies of 4, combined with the

nourishing potential of the 8 Earth, indicates considerable motivation toward compassion and interest in taking care of others – but only when the mountain is inclined and not stricken by the aloof or detached part of his character!

In relationships, this person would do well to draw on his deeper resources of judgement – the 8 and 4 reserves – when making important choices or when taking major decisions and actions. Coming from the 9 nature in such matters, such as falling in love with someone and wanting to marry them on the spur of the moment, would not be a good idea – but he might think of it.

ABOVE: *You can begin to unravel the mysterious nature of love through Feng Shui Astrology.*

In communication, he needs to be aware that the merits of his well-thought-out arguments, plans, and visions will not always be quite so self-evident to those with less insight. So he should take care to spell things out – without arrogance, if possible. Communication about his wants, needs, and feelings will also require special effort in any intimate relationship. But his capacity for commitment, concentrated persistence, and focus can help make the right relationship something really special.

CHAPTER THREE

Understanding Your Lover

I N CHAPTER TWO, *you discovered how to work out your own Feng Shui Astrology chart, summarized in the three key numbers that symbolize the influences operating at the time of your birth. In this chapter, you will see how to apply the same principles to another person, with some shortcuts and guidelines for different situations. The steps set out in this chapter also serve as a convenient step-by-step summary of those set out in the previous one.*

You may wish to use this information in a number of different ways. For instance, you might want to gain a better insight into the astrological make-up of someone with whom you're already in a relationship; in this case, the information here may help you understand seeming contradictions within the other person's personality or behavior; for there are many influences at work in all of us. Or it could help you get a perspective on which patterns within that person are major and fundamental and which are more trivial or superficial; this can often make it easier to make the most of your relationship.

Alternatively, you may want to quickly gain an evaluation of the likely nature of someone you've just met – information which will help you get to know the person that bit more quickly, profoundly,

ABOVE: *If there is a person out there waiting for you, how will you recognize them?*

and painlessly. For example, you may wish to know in advance how they are likely to express their sexuality. Might intimacy be daunting for them? Are they likely to be strong on commitment? Or might they want to have half a dozen other lovers in tow, as well as yourself? Will they turn out to be the sort of person that can keep deep, dark secrets from you for years and years? Examining their Magic Square chart can provide a lot of these answers quickly.

Thirdly, maybe you haven't anyone in mind just at the moment and simply want to have some indications in order to narrow down your particular field a bit! This may not sound like the most reliable way to approach the search for a deep and meaningful soulmate relationship, but I do recommend it as a good way for you to practice using this astrological method – tuning into the

astrological influences at work, learning to distinguish the different types. This will not only help you develop your intuitive ability for creating better relationships and knowing your

ABOVE: *Do you both want the same thing? The Magic Square can provide some revealing answers.*

partner better, but it will also sensitize you to the energies at work in your own life. Various different suggestions for following up on this approach are given at the end of this chapter.

WORKING OUT YOUR LOVER'S CHART

STEP 1

Obtain the birth-date

(by fair means or foul!)

STEP 2

Work out the Primary Number

Fortunately, there is a very simple formula you can use to work this out, without consulting any charts or tables. Just follow these steps:

✳ Add together the four digits of the year of birth

✳ If this new number is greater than ten, add its two digits together to produce a single-figure number, e.g.

$$1947$$
$$1 + 9 + 4 + 7 = 21$$
$$2 + 1 = 3$$

✳ Subtract this number from 11, and you get the primary number. e.g. for

$$1947$$
$$11 - 3 = 8$$

However, always remember that the Oriental year for this purpose begins on February 4, not January 1. So if the birth-date is between January 1 and February 3 it belongs in the previous year.

STEP 3

Work out the Inner Number

Look down the column in the chart below which contains your Primary Number at the top and read off your number matching the day of the month you were born.

BIRTH-DATE	PRIMARY NUMBER		
	1 OR 4 OR 7	2 OR 5 OR 8	3 OR 6 OR 9
FEBRUARY 4 TO MARCH 5	8	2	5
MARCH 6 TO APRIL 4	7	1	4
APRIL 5 TO MAY 5	6	9	3
MAY 6 TO JUNE 5	5	8	2
JUNE 6 TO JULY 7	4	7	1
JULY 8 TO AUGUST 7	3	6	9
AUGUST 8 TO SEPTEMBER 7	2	5	8
SEPTEMBER 8 TO OCTOBER 8	1	4	7
OCTOBER 9 TO NOVEMBER 7	9	3	6
NOVEMBER 8 TO DECEMBER 7	8	2	5
DECEMBER 8 TO JANUARY 5	7	1	4
JANUARY 6 TO FEBRUARY 3	6	9	3

STEP 4

Work out the Outer Number

Find the square that has your Inner Number in the center. Look for the position in the square occupied by your Primary Number. Now look at the central square and find the number that occupies the same position. This is your Outer Number.

STEP 5

Interpret the numbers

You now have a three-number chart for the person you have in mind, such as 8:4:9 or 2:2:5. The Primary Number represents the way the nine types of influence appear in the person's "constitutional" nature and sexuality – the major influences on how he or she lives life in the world. The Inner Number represents the qualities not usually so evident in worldly life – the more private, spiritual nature, and the inner force.

The Outer Number represents the aspects that are most outward or "on the surface" and how one expresses oneself in behavior and habits.

3	8	1
2	4	6
7	9	5

8	4	6
7	9	2
3	5	1

1	6	8
9	2	4
5	7	3

2	7	9
1	3	5
6	8	4

4	9	2
3	5	7
8	1	6

6	2	4
5	7	9
1	3	8

7	3	5
6	8	1
2	4	9

9	5	7
8	1	3
4	6	2

5	1	3
4	6	8
9	2	7

RIGHT: *Understanding the Feng Shui Astrological make-up of your partner will help you to build a more intimate relationship.*

THE NINE CHARACTER TYPES

1. MOVING WATER
ELEMENT: WATER

Readiness for motion, patience in difficulties, ability to get round obstacles, creating one's own path in life, independence, potential for obstinacy, hardworking, aptitude for concentration, intuitive, uses emotional depths, is sociable – but can enjoy solitude, strong sexual desires, apparent emotional coolness, carefulness, can worry unnecessarily, get in a rut, usually gets there in the end.

2. THE EARTH
ELEMENT: EARTH

Receptivity, dedication, nourishing, supportive, quiet and effective action, often reserved and gentle, sense of service, can be self-sacrificing, motherly or feminine quality, perceptive of others' needs, harmonious, diligent, interested in completing things, tact and diplomacy, modesty, stronger on ideals and aspirations than on practicalities, good on detail, can be insecure.

3. THUNDER
ELEMENT: WOOD

Explosive energy, brightness, and vibrancy, active vitality, outgoing, generally irrepressible and optimistic, needing sense of progress, restless quest for experience and experiment, curious, interested in growth, can be hasty or rash, quick to change, unpredictable, short tempered, superficial,

ABOVE: *If you're eager to get going and able to clear any obstacles in your path, you're a typical number 1 "Water" type.*

ABOVE: *Don't undermine your caring and supportive "Earth" nature by being overly self-sacrificing.*

overlooking practicalities, impatient, varied talents, aesthetic values, sensual pleasures, romantic, acute sensitivity, especially enjoying sound and music, easily hurt, frank.

4. THE WIND
ELEMENT: WOOD

Strong sense of movement in life, many changes, scattering of energy, talkative, good at communicating and disseminating information, mental ability, quick at perception, intuition, often charismatic, impulsive, influenced by emotion, affectionate and romantic, can be impractical in love, naive, subject to changes of mind and influence of others, indecision can cause

confusion and threaten usual confidence, moodiness, artistically oriented, adaptable and able to bounce back from any failure.

5. CENTRAL POWER
ELEMENT: EARTH

Being at the center of things, organizer of others, forceful, enjoying power, loves influence and responsibility, egotism, boldness, controlling self and others, has both creative and destructive ability, openness to extreme experiences, can have an inner reconciliation of opposites, seeming emotional self-sufficiency, endures hardships, insensitive to others' vulnerability and needs.

ABOVE: *The vibrant energy, sensitivity, and aesthetic nature of the ballerina is typical of number 3 "Thunder" types.*

ABOVE: *"Central Power" types like to lead the way and be in control, even at the expense of others' feelings.*

6. HEAVEN

ELEMENT: METAL

Order, constancy, dignity, perfection, courage, discipline, inner strength, discipline and organization, clarity of purpose, seeking completeness, willpower, leadership, high ideals, pride, exemplary behavior, reliability, intellect, independence, rigidity, calculating mind, ability to dominate, self-esteem, not enjoying subordinate position, can be manipulative, slow to take advice or criticism, emotionally cool, inwardly turned rather than sociable, able to accumulate material possessions.

7. HARVEST

ELEMENT: METAL

Material and financial acquisitions, enjoyment of spending, resourcefulness, competence, hard work

before relaxation, seeking enjoyment, easygoing, values freedom, sharp mind, good adviser, confident, respectful, loyal, talks rather than listens, writing, persuasive, self-interested, strong outside, cautious inside, changeable temperament, outward appearances important, show-off, strong passions and attractions, sexual relations very important, most productive in later life.

8. THE MOUNTAIN

ELEMENT: EARTH

Enjoying stability, self-reflective, strength of mind, immovable, stubborn, high-minded, far-reaching perspective, self-motivated, tenacious, orderly and patient, may hide emotions and desires, not verbally expressive, cautious in relationship: faithful, steady and trustworthy, able to accumulate wealth.

ABOVE: *Courage, willpower, and clarity of purpose are just some of the high ideals important to number 6 "Heaven" types.*

ABOVE: *Number 7 types enjoy relaxing after a hard day's work, as well as spending their well-earned wages.*

9. FIRE

ELEMENT: FIRE

Bright intelligence, flamboyance, energy in bursts, emptiness after exhaustion, quick changes of emotion, outgoing and sociable, keen on fame and success, concerned with attractiveness, enjoying involvement in things, wide circle of contacts, versatile, keen to communicate, impulsive, can be vain, disliking constraints, "cheerleader" potential.

Remember that these are broad influences, which will show up in slightly different ways in different individuals, so bear this in mind in your interpretation. Also bear in mind that few people will appreciate you working out their numbers, then marching up to them and blithely announcing who you think they are. In practice, most people don't enjoy being pigeon-holed, even if you're assigning them fantastic qualities. Probably better to keep your findings to yourself for the time being – and even then, remain open-minded.

Finally, remember the three different ways in which the three numbers show up. For instance, if you interact with someone daily, but never talk about anything more important that the weather, what you see is probably their Primary Number at work. If you've never met someone before and you're going on first impressions, it's probably their Outer Number influence you're experiencing. If the two of you go way back, then you're getting glimpses of their Inner Number state.

ABOVE: *Life with your "Mountain" partner may be stable and comfortable – but watch out for that stubborn streak!*

ABOVE: *You'll never know when your "Fire" partner might flare up next, but life with him or her will never be dull!*

LEARNING TO RECOGNIZE TYPES

YOU HAVE learned first how to recognize which of the Five Elements and the nine influences are at work in your own life. Now, perhaps, you have also been able to experiment with interpreting the charts of a number of people you know reasonably well. If so, you'll begin to get a real feeling for how these influences show up in people around you. Then you might find yourself beginning to guess at which elements and which numbers are at play in the individuals around you, without knowing their birth data. Not only is this fun, and not only might it help you meet someone you'd like to get to know a whole lot better – but it's also an excellent way of tuning into the whole system and developing your sensitivity to the factors at work.

So wherever you are, you can find opportunities to practice this. Spotting the elements is a good way to start. At work, for instance, you may come to realize that your long-time boss, who is terribly well organized but has never given much away about what's going on inside, is actually showing Metal influence. At your favorite nightclub, you might recognize that your favorite high-energy-but-only-in-bursts DJ is a classic example of Fire energy. In the bar, that gentle-looking person who's been quietly giving you the eye for a while, but not doing much about it just yet, may well be of the Earth species.

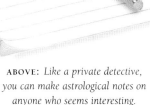

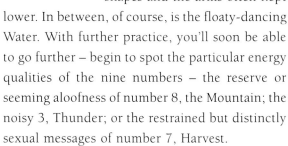

ABOVE: *Like a private detective, you can make astrological notes on anyone who seems interesting.*

In fact, the kind of places where you might want to go to meet someone new are ideal for this sort of practice. All the information is there – the way a person sits or stands, indeed their whole body language; how they interact with those around them; their vocal expression (watery? fiery? metallic?). These, and many more, are the clues to the elements at work.

Take the way people dance, for instance – one of the most revealing indicators of all. Look at the people on the dance floor. First of all, practice sorting the Yins from the Yangs; which ones are moving with more "up" energy and which more "down?" This is the first clue. Then break it down further; start spotting the elements. Fire style dancing tends to be the wildest, most communicative and exhibitionistic. Wood dancers also have a strong upward energy, with a more steady, irrepressible flow. On the other side, Earth dancing has a more subdued quality; Metal tends to be more self-contained, the body taking more compact shapes and the arms often kept lower. In between, of course, is the floaty-dancing Water. With further practice, you'll soon be able to go further – begin to spot the particular energy qualities of the nine numbers – the reserve or seeming aloofness of number 8, the Mountain; the noisy 3, Thunder; or the restrained but distinctly sexual messages of number 7, Harvest.

SPOT THE TYPES

After you have been practicing Feng Shui Astrology for a while, you will find that you pick up an instinct for spotting the influences at work in those around you. This is a good party trick, but it is also a sign that you are sensitive to the way the complex of types and elements works.

ABOVE: *Someone you know quite well, like your boss, should be easy to identify.*

ABOVE: *If you know a person's talents, you can probably work out their element.*

ABOVE: *Even a complete stranger will give tell-tale signs to the experienced observer.*

After a while, you'll find that this whole process will become less analytical and you'll naturally be picking up on a "certain something," that very particular energy quality that characterizes each number. So there you are – a blind date need never be quite so unnerving again!

CHAPTER FOUR

Are We Compatible?

N OW YOU HAVE *worked out the set of three Magic Square numbers for yourself and for your lover, partner, soul-mate – or potential candidate for the job. From these figures, you have interpreted many indicators of personality, relationship potential, and general approach to life, for you both. This in itself contains many indicators of potential compatibility, and will already have given you some clues about the dynamics of your interaction. For instance, one of you may be a wildly hedonistic party animal, whilst the other is a shy, retiring hermit whose main interest is spiritual withdrawal from the sensorial world.*

This sort of comparison is simply common sense and is based upon a straightforward sense of judgement – which, of course, is very important in astrological investigation.

Whether you wish to further understand an existing relationship or check out the possibilities of a projected one, however, the Magic Square system of Feng Shui Astrology goes a lot further than this.

It offers some simple, powerful, and fascinating techniques for more specifically analysing the interacting of the energies of two individuals whose numbers are known. These methods derive from the same body of Oriental wisdom as the study of the nine influences themselves; so they too have come down to us from thousands of years of use both in classical China and its Asiatic zones of influence.

ABOVE: *The eyes may be "the window of the soul' but Feng Shui Astrology can tell you more!*

Compatibility has many different aspects – sexual compatibility, romantic preferences, communication patterns, social preferences, basic lifestyle compatibility, even broad outlook on life – and many other matters that govern how the individual will function in intimacy and familiarity with another. All these aspects together form a web of interactive elements, the overall pattern and underlying dynamic of which can be profoundly illuminated by carrying out Magic Square analysis. Again, it's important to remember, as in chapter one where personal characteristics were interpreted, that

you will find it most helpful to gain an understanding of how your two personalities are likely to react to one another at the level of cosmic energies; then you will be able to make a creative and personalized interpretation based on what you know about the two people in question. This will be a lot more accurate than just taking literally the guide-

ABOVE: *Compatibility is determined at a cosmic level.*

lines set out here. To give you an idea, some examples of real people will be worked through, after the methods described on the next few pages.

The first step is to get a broad view of the overall energies contained within your relationship, and this is gained by carrying out a simple Yin/Yang analysis on the interaction of your charts. To do this we will have to use what we have already learned.

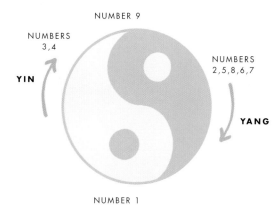

ABOVE: With the right balance of Yin and Yang, your relationship will really take off!

You will recall that the numbers 2, 5 and 8 (Earth) and 6 and 7 (Metal) represent the more Yang, downward, and counteractive side of the ongoing cycle of transformation of energies in the earth's atmosphere; that numbers 9 (Fire) and 3 and 4 (Wood) express the more Yin, upward, and expansive energies; whilst number 1 (Water) denotes the transitional state in between.

The combination of Yin and Yang components can be studied by comparing your two charts. Let's take an example of two people:

PERSON A – 8:4:9
PERSON B – 7:1:2

✳ First of all, let's look at them individually. Person A has a Yang Primary Number, but a Yin Inner and Outer Number. Person B also has a Yang Primary Number, but with a neutral Inner Number and Yang Outer Number. In a Yin-and-Yang "balance sheet" for the couple, there's a little more Yang energy than Yin.

✳ We can also compare them in terms of their three personality departments. In primary nature – fundamental nature, sexual expression, and so on – they are both on the Yang side, and they will have this point in common, creating empathy. In Inner Number and spirituality, Person A is more Yin than Person B, who is neutral.

✳ In more superficial aspects, Person B is more Yang and Person A more Yin. These latter two variations of their basic "energetic polarity" will enhance their potential relationship, broadening the spectrum of the interactions of their energies. This is something to bear in mind as a background to the more detailed analysis that follows.

THE THREE LEVELS
OF COMPATIBILITY

COMPATIBILITY CAN be assessed at a number of different levels or stages. Each of these takes into account how your energies interact in the different personality categories represented by the three numbers – primary expression in life including sexuality, inner personality or driving force, and outer behavioral patterns. These stages

LEFT: *A relationship can be enhanced where there is a strong Yin/Yang variation.*

ABOVE: *Unlikely combinations can work out well if the universal energies are complementary.*

of the analysis follow the same steps which were used when assessing the individual. The first level looks at compatibility in simple Yin/Yang terms; the

next stage is to examine the interaction of the elements involved; the third is to look at how the nine Magic Square influences will combine.

Traditional Chinese interpretation of these factors often comes up with a very hard-and-fast set of combinations, which are rigidly classified as "auspicious" or "inauspicious." But this old-style approach is based on certain unspoken criteria, rooted in a very traditional society that was extremely stable and lasted a long time. Nowadays, we may be more prepared to look at relationships, including the challenges presented, with a view to making it all work better, rather than deterministically saying that this relationship simply won't work and this other one will – with no place for the operation of free will and effort. Besides, certain combinations might work in post-feminist industrial society that simply wouldn't in rural ancient China. Let's now look at these three levels of compatibility analysis in more detail.

FIVE ELEMENT COMPATIBILITY

THE NEXT STEP is to break down the different influences that are at work in the two individuals and look at which elements feature in your two charts, and how they will be interacting. This provides information about the most powerful influences on compatibility. Each person's chart of three numbers will comprise up to three different elements.

To understand how these element influences interact, we must go back and look again at the cycle of Five Elements that was introduced in chapter one. In this circle of relationship, each element has a distinctly different relationship with each of the other elements, and each of these types of connection implies a different quality in terms of compatibility. The interactions of the elements follow two basic patterns, which are known as the cycle of support and the cycle of control.

ABOVE: As with the interactions of the elements, our relationships are based on the cycles of support and control.

THE CYCLE OF SUPPORT

This interrelationship is based upon the progressive cycle of the elements, as exemplified by the natural cycle of the seasons, and its implications can be understood from the way this works in nature. Deep winter turns into spring, but in its dormancy preparations are already going on below the surface, for the buds that later burst forth and the bulbs that shoot up. The growth of spring already contains the nascent buds that will later blossom as summer approaches. The flowers

ABOVE: *Even as snow lies on the ground, Yin energies are once again gathering for the cycle of growth.*

Translating this into the terms of the classical Five Elements, then:

Water provides the essential element for wood to grow

✳

Wood provides the fuel for fire to burn

✳

Fire provides ash that nourishes the earth

✳

Earth provides the ore that makes metal

✳

Metal melts into the fluid state of water

We see that each element is supported by the element preceding it and supports that which follows it in the ongoing cycle of transformation.

contain preparations for the fruit to set soon, in early fall, and the fruit contains the embryonic seeds that come to the fore in later fall. The fall processes, in their turn, prepare for the renewed dormancy of next winter. Thus each stage supports or prepares for the next, and is dependent upon the preparations made in the previous stage for its own lifecycle to succeed.

THE CYCLE OF CONTROL

THIS IS THE OTHER side of the coin, representing the other force in nature – the way that
certain energies limit or destroy others, so that
nature's cycle of birth, death, and rebirth continues
and maintains a state of dynamic balance, rather
than endlessly increasing. Just as the forces of Yin
and Yang have their interaction of opposition, each
element has a relationship of inhibition with
another two, balancing its supporting relationship
to the two others. So each element limits one other
and is limited by yet another; and these are the two
elements that are found on the opposite side of the
cycle. This set of control relationships also proceeds
continuously in an ever-continuing cycle, main-
taining the balance and making each element
equally important, equally powerful, and totally
integrated into the whole, elegant pattern.

ABOVE: *The constant cycle of opposing
energies ensures continuity and balance.*

BELOW: *Fire can destroy, but also
clears the way for new growth.*

THE CONTROL CYCLE

FIRE
NUMBER
9

WOOD
NUMBERS
3 & 4

EARTH
NUMBERS
2, 5 & 8

WATER
NUMBER
1

METAL
NUMBERS
6 & 7

Water can extinguish fire

✳

Fire can melt metal

✳

Metal can cut wood

✳

**Wood can penetrate earth,
as the roots of trees**

✳

**Earth can contain water,
as the banks of rivers and lakes**

This circle of elements produces the classic star-shaped pattern that is imposed on the circular pattern of the support cycle of the elements. This gives a control cycle which not only has an equally powerful effect on how two people are going to relate to one another but, in a wider sense, illustrates the self-regulation of intrinsic natural forces that the natural world uses in order to keep everything in balance.

APPLYING THE FIVE ELEMENT ANALYSIS

N OW YOU CAN COMPARE your elements with those of the other person, in the three departments – overall personality, inner nature, and surface nature. Of these, the elemental comparison of your two Primary Numbers is traditionally regarded as being the most powerful aspect in terms of compatibility. For each figure in your chart, the other person's number will fall into one of the categories set out below in relation to your own:

* the same element
* the supporting element
* the supported element
* the controlling element
* the controlled element

When your two elements have a supporting connection, this is traditionally considered a good basis for a harmonious relationship. There is a measure of polarity, which creates attraction, but enough affinity to make for ease of communication and empathy.

If your two elements have a controlling connection, this is traditionally considered less harmonious and less compatible, but adds a component of the attraction of elemental opposites.

ABOVE: Number 9 "Fire" types should seek out the balancing elements of Wood and Earth in their lives.

There may be excitement and variety galore, but communication, goal-sharing, and understanding of one another is not easy.

If you share the same element, you will probably have a great deal in common and feel great empathy for one another, but there may not be such a strong "spark" due to lack of polarity. This combination usually has a very stable quality – perhaps too stable. This is traditionally reckoned to indicate moderate compatibility.

Again, you can look first at which elements are present in the total combination of your

ABOVE: The interaction of your two primary elements is the most important factor for compatibility.

WORKED EXAMPLE

Let's look again at the case which has already been analysed in terms of Yin and Yang balance.

PERSON A

| EARTH | WOOD | FIRE |

PERSON B

| METAL | WATER | EARTH |

ABOVE: *This combination of numbers should ensure a strong and successful relationship.*

ELEMENT CONTENT OF COMBINED CHARTS

This combination of charts incorporates at least one incidence of every single element – with Earth occurring twice – which indicates a healthy breadth of energies and expression existing in the relationship as a whole. Many relationships have a more predominant presence of a smaller range of elements, which will tend to narrow the range of energies and expression of the relationship as a whole. In terms of primary elements, Earth and Metal will be the most prominent in this relationship's energies.

DETAILED ELEMENT ANALYSIS

PRIMARY NUMBERS
✳ In terms of their primary nature, Person A's Earth supports Person B's Metal

INNER NUMBERS
✳ In terms of underlying nature, Person B's Water supports Person A's Wood

OUTER NUMBERS
✳ In terms of outer nature, Person A's Fire supports Person B's Earth

Overall then, there is a high degree of classic compatibility, for all three numbers involve a support connection. Person B receives the greater part of the flow of support energies, but both parties benefit from the compatibility.

two charts, and then check out the more profound aspect of how you both relate to each other in your three respective departments – overall personality, inner, and outer nature.

Finally, you can bring the whole picture together and draw some overall conclusions as to the potential relationship that lies ahead: whether it's worth the effort or a definite non-starter.

ELEMENT COMBINATIONS
FOR LOVE, SEX, AND ROMANCE

WATER + WATER

SINGLE ELEMENT COMBINATION

✻ Romance and sex may have a shallow dimension, due to lack of polarity

✻ Need to cultivate their inherent differences to maintain the spark and keep their romance alive

WATER + WOOD

SUPPORT CYCLE COMBINATION

✻ Similarity in their mode of sexuality, neither pressurizing the other too much

✻ Able to attune to each other instinctively

WATER + FIRE

CONTROL CYCLE COMBINATION

✻ Initial passion, but Fire may prove too fast, furious, and self-centered for Water

✻ Needs adaptation on both sides to survive as a relationship

WATER + EARTH

CONTROL CYCLE COMBINATION

✻ Differences in erotic energies – floating and flowing versus down-to-earth groundedness

✻ Need to make efforts to stay in touch, especially in terms of feelings

WATER + METAL

SUPPORT CYCLE COMBINATION

✻ Can understand each other easily enough

✻ Need to tolerate each other's differing romantic styles – Water likes to go with the flow, Metal likes to be in charge and call the tune; dictating the course of true love

WOOD + WOOD

SINGLE ELEMENT COMBINATION

✻ Strong romantic content, but not so much sexual polarity

✻ Need to pursue their own distinctive paths – and allow the other to do the same

WOOD + FIRE

SUPPORT CYCLE COMBINATION

* Opposite natures, but can work well sexually
* Need to be clear about their own differing individual needs

WOOD + EARTH

CONTROL CYCLE COMBINATION

* Attraction of opposites, but conflicting social and expressive preferences may give rise to alienation
* Need to tolerate these differences

WOOD + METAL

CONTROL CYCLE COMBINATION

* Wood's lightness can be suppressed by Metal's control
* Need to accept each other's differing basic outlook on life

FIRE + FIRE

SINGLE ELEMENT COMBINATION

* Strong in the beginning – sudden passion, varied and inventive love-making
* Need to take care that it doesn't end just as suddenly as it began

LEFT: *Fire and Metal: sexual attraction may be complicated by the battle for individual expression.*

FIRE + EARTH

SUPPORT CYCLE COMBINATION

* Reasonable potential for passion
* Good at meeting each other's needs and coping with the differences

FIRE + METAL

CONTROL CYCLE COMBINATION

* Erotic attraction, but can be a battle of wills; Fire can make Metal feel powerless
* Both need to give the other space, and have their own life, as well as the relationship

EARTH + EARTH

SINGLE ELEMENT COMBINATION

* Strong on physical and sensual compatibility
* Can lack sexual adventurousness

EARTH + METAL

SUPPORT CYCLE COMBINATION

* Can adapt to each other easily
* Love and sex can be enhanced by their different approaches

METAL + METAL

SINGLE ELEMENT COMBINATION

* Lots of sexuality and passion; struggle to see who's boss
* Needs dedication and give-and-take

NINE-NUMBER COMPATIBILITY

ANALYSIS OF THE interaction of the nine specific influences within your relationship brings the final component to your examination, and can add uncanny and compelling insights. In this form of analysis, too, there are strongly-held traditional ideas about which numbers are most compatible, especially Primary Number combinations. There is certainly a sound basis for these conventional views, even if they should be interpreted with some discrimination rather than regarded as inviolable and carved in stone.

The additional factor that comes into play here is the respective positions in the Magic Square occupied by your numbers from each of the three personality categories. This is superimposed over the very powerful influence of the element

4	9	2
3	5	7
8	1	6

ABOVE: The standard magic square.

combinations which we have just examined. Adding these two factors together produces the following set of assessments.

ABOVE: Which should I go for – sexy, reliable, or sensitive? Choice should not be based on tradition alone.

The numbers which are traditionally considered most compatible with yours are those connected as supporting elements, plus the number that is directly opposite on the Magic Square. These are traditionally regarded as the most powerfully attracting numbers, and their energetic connection can override or mask the limiting influence of the control cycle. This creates the strongest pull of all between human beings, and is found at the basis of many celebrated romances, such as John and Jackie Kennedy and John Lennon and Yoko Ono. In the truly mystical nature of numbers, you can easily work out the attracting number that corresponds to yours by simply subtracting your own Primary Number from ten. However, it must be remembered that this is an energy that pulls two people toward one another, and is not enough on

4	9	2
3	5	7
8	1	6

4	9	2
3	5	7
8	1	6

ABOVE: *To work out the attracting number that corresponds with yours, just subtract your own Primary Number from ten.*

its own to make a relationship work. There generally need to be elements of harmony and communication as well.

The number combinations considered reasonably compatible with yours are those that are the same number or the same element as yours – unless the latter happens to be your attracting number, lying on the opposite corner of the Magic Square.

The numbers traditionally reckoned to be least compatible with yours are those which are connected in the control cycle – unless this happens to be your attracting number.

Lastly, we can also look at the specific number combinations that occur in the other two departments, bearing in mind that these will represent a less fundamental indicator. Having the same Inner Number, for instance, can be an extremely powerful enhancement in a relationship, for it makes for profound communication abilities and mutual understanding. Sharing the same Outer Number can also be a lesser benefit, because it indicates having similar habits and outer traits. Each of these can be more advantageous when there is a positive dynamic between the Primary Numbers but works against you if not.

NUMBER	MOST COMPATIBLE	MODERATELY COMPATIBLE	LEAST COMPATIBLE
1	34679	1	258
2	6789	25	134
3	179	34	2568
4	169	34	2578
5	679	258	134
6	2458	67	39
7	2358	67	49
8	2679	58	134
9	123458	9	67

ABOVE: *Choose your new partner with care! If the above numbers indicate only moderate compatibility, be prepared to work a little harder in the relationship.*

LEFT: *When the most auspicious combination of numbers combine, the attraction is irresistible and enduring, as with John Lennon and Yoko Ono.*

THE FAMILY ROLES
OF THE NINE NUMBERS

ONE FURTHER criterion can be added. Each number carries an archetypal "family" role, which has been evolved in the symbolism of the trigrams from the *I Ching*; and so you can gain additional understanding of the interaction of your Primary Number with another by bringing together your two "family types" – see the box directly below.

ABOVE: *In ancient Chinese wisdom, each number symbolizes a specific family "type."*

Thus, for example, in the case in question, Person A's number 8 is associated with the youngest daughter, while Person B's number 7 represents the youngest son. So even as they grow old, this couple will always have something of the

1	Middle son
2	Mother
3	Eldest son
4	Eldest daughter
5	Seventh child
6	Youngest son
7	Father
8	Youngest daughter
9	Middle daughter

dynamic of the young brother and sister. For instance, they will be able to benefit from others' experiences, learn from other people who have pioneered a field of progress, enjoy being taken care of – and enjoy having this in common with one another. Let's now apply this whole process of compatibility testing to a well-known case in the panel opposite.

Remember – looking at astrological compatibility isn't about whether certain relationships are "good" or "bad." When combinations of energies are naturally harmonious, this is to be taken advantage of; when they aren't, you can better understand the nature of the conflicting energies that need to be recognized, addressed, and assimilated. Besides, even the most stable and harmonious relationship contains conflict, and that isn't a bad thing – in fact, it's probably essential. The trick is to understand the nature of such interacting energies in order to understand what you're dealing with; then you can take steps to make things work better; to work with what you've got. That's what the following chapter is all about.

ABOVE: *An attraction of opposites did not make up for the lack of mutual elements and support in this marriage.*

✳ Charles was born on November 14th, 1948, so his numbers are 7:8:4.

✳ Diana was born on July 1st, 1961, so her numbers were 3:1:7.

CHARLES

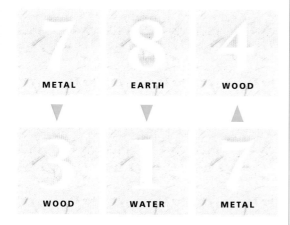

METAL	EARTH	WOOD
▼	▼	▲
WOOD	WATER	METAL

DIANA

Now we compare these sets of numbers. As shown here, the most striking feature is that there were no elements in common, nor supporting element combinations – everything was based on inhibiting or control dynamics.

ANALYSIS

In terms of overall Yin/Yang analysis, Charles' make-up is more predominantly Yang, grounded, and inwardly-turned. Diana's chart had more Yin energies, making for lightness and outgoingness.

Now, looking at their three personality categories individually, we see that in terms of both overall personality and inner or spiritual nature, Charles had the more dominant and controlling energies, whereas in the realm of superficial appearances and immediate effects, Diana had the upper hand. Anyone in Diana's position might understandably have suffered from this degree of control in the two more fundamental life areas; she might also have been tempted to use her power in the third category to try to redress the balance. At least she could get some benefit from this; when Charles did the same, it wasn't so successful an exercise. When they battled in the realm of the Outer Numbers, Diana was sure to win.

OPPOSITES ATTRACT

In their relationship, there was clearly also a large degree of the attraction of opposites. In fact, they were an excellent example of attracting Primary Numbers – in this case 7 and 3. Sadly, it seems that this attraction of opposites did not make up for the lack of aspects in common or potential for support, which clearly contributed to the demise of the relationship. In terms of family-role numbers, Diana was the eldest son, while Charles is the youngest son, which may go some way to explain how Diana could often seem to be the one with the more dominant persona.

CHAPTER FIVE

Getting the Relationship to Work

B Y NOW YOU'VE *thoroughly checked out the prospects for your relationship. As you've seen, some combinations offer distinctly more straightforward compatibility than others; but even the least fortuitous combination is workable and even the most fortunate will not work without effort. Of course, all relationships require certain basic input, such as commitment, communication, desire, expression of affection, preservation of personal identity, and sheer investment of time and effort. However, some of these inputs will prove particularly crucial in some types of combination, some in others. Some will mean harder work than others.*

ABOVE: *Even where number combinations are not ideal, Feng Shui Astrology can show you how to bring out the best in your relationship.*

Broadly speaking, the classically less compatible relationships, characterized by strongly antagonizing energies, will require strong and constant efforts to bridge the gaps, while the more placid combinations of kindred spirits will need to work at avoiding blandness. Even the more ideal combinations that lie between these extremes may well require a mixture of both strategies. A great deal of what it takes to make a relationship work is common sense, but Feng Shui Astrology can add particular direction and specific guidance, using the subtle interactions of the Five Elements and the nine influences to maximize the potential and minimize the shortcomings of any couple.

Such strategies can be found at a number of levels. First of all, it's fruitful to consider steps you can take personally to deal with the tendencies of

your inherent nature; especially those qualities that will most directly affect your prospects in love, sex, romance, and relationships – whoever you're with. Then you can go on to examine measures that will improve the prospects of your particular relationship, first in terms of element combinations, and then in interactions of the nine influences or types.

ABOVE: *Don't despair if your numbers aren't compatible! Mutual support and interaction will make a big difference.*

GETTING IT RIGHT

Feng Shui Astrology can add direction and guidance to improve any relationship – but first, a solid base:

✳ Consider steps you can take to deal with your inherent nature. This will be especially true of those features directly affecting your prospects in love, sex, and romance.

✳ Next, concentrate on, and improve, the prospects of any given relationship. Firstly in terms of element combinations, and then in interactions of the nine influences or types.

DEVELOPING YOUR OWN
POTENTIAL FOR RELATIONSHIP

The first factor in any relationship with another person is your relationship with yourself. Clichéd, certainly – but true. If you're happy and fulfilled in yourself, then you're obviously going to be a better person with whom to be in relationship; you're going to choose lovers more wisely; and you're going to be better at getting a relationship to work.

Feng Shui Astrology offers a special opportunity to give structure to this, with emphasis on the qualities that will most affect your intimate interaction with another human being. So the first thing to do is to look again at the inherent qualities of your Primary Number, and then cultivate approaches that reduce any detrimental effect.

Suggestions are given below.

NUMBER 1
Insecure * Can worry unnecessarily *
Doesn't want to cause any trouble
Easily swayed * Others can't tell
what you're feeling

LEFT: *You have to like yourself first to be successful in your relationships with others.*

NUMBER 2
Conservative tendency * Can be reticent *
Sometimes self-sacrificing *
Stronger on ideals and aspirations
than seeing things through

NUMBER 3
Ambitious * Independent
Can be rash or hasty * Sensitive and easily hurt *
Unpredictable and quick to change *
Sometimes overwhelming or brutally frank

NUMBER 4
Acting on impulse * Changeable and indecisive *
Turbulent emotions * Confusion, lack of clarity,
or single-mindedness *
Can be taken in by the unscrupulous

NUMBER 5
Given to extremes * Can be tactless *
Needs to be the centre of attention *
Can be controlling, manipulative, or inconsiderate *
Not strong on expressing own emotional
needs or softer side

NUMBER 6

Stubborn ✳ Cool or reserved ✳
Can be calculating ✳ Focuses strongly on self ✳
Likes to dominate a relationship ✳
Rigidity, pride, and inflexible will

NUMBER 7

Hedonistic ✳ Self-interested ✳
Can easily feel constrained ✳ May be arrogant ✳
Moods can oscillate widely ✳
Nervous about commitment

NUMBER 8

Stubborn ✳ Resistant to change ✳
Prone to isolation ✳ High self-esteem and ego ✳
Can be hard to get to know ✳
Haughty, aloof, or distant-seeming

NUMBER 9

Impatient ✳ Lack of self-control ✳
Can be inconstant ✳ May be fickle or vain ✳
Trouble with long-term commitment ✳
Easily influenced by stronger individuals

USING THE FIVE ELEMENTS

IT IS ALSO WORTH WHILE, in the interests of better relationships, to explore your own personal life expression in terms of the Five Elements. First, make sure you are truly expressing your native element. If your Primary Number is 9, for instance, make sure your Fire nature is getting expressed and lived through in your lifestyle, activities, career and work, hobbies, and so on, rather than being suppressed. You might want to look

	FIRE	Include Wood and Earth patterns in your life expression
	EARTH	Include Metal and Fire patterns in your life expression
	METAL	Include Water and Earth patterns in your life expression
	WATER	Include Wood and Metal patterns in your life expression
	WOOD	include Fire and Water patterns in your life expression

BELOW: *Are you expressing your true element in your everyday life? This is an important step in improving your relationships.*

back to the information contained in chapter one, if you need to refresh your memory and pick up some pointers for the way ahead.

Secondly, acquaint yourself with the nature of the two elements that naturally complement yours – those which lie on either side of yours on the Five Element support cycle. Make sure you are capable,

SUPPORTING ELEMENTS

Always remember the support
cycle of the five elements.

**Water provides the essential
element for wood to grow**

✳

**Wood provides the fuel
for fire to burn**

✳

**Fire provides ash that
nourishes the earth**

✳

**Earth provides the ore
that makes metal**

✳

**Metal melts into the fluid
state of water**

Making the most of this interaction of the
elements will strengthen the supportive side of
your relationships.

ABOVE: *Understand and express your true self –
and allow your partner to do the same.*

in your life expression, of also on occasion overlapping into the territory represented by them; for this is a natural part of your inherent potential. The corresponding elements are shown opposite.

Broadly speaking, the limitations described on the previous pages, signifying your lower potential for self-expression and relating, correspond to qualities associated with your missing two elements – those that relate to yours on the control cycle.

COMING TO TERMS WITH YOURSELF

Finally, consider your three-number make-up. This is a classic summary of your "relationship with yourself." If you can manage to fully integrate these diverse aspects, including any conflicting tendencies in terms of elements, then your potential for relationships will be so much better. Understanding and expressing your true self, combined with flexibility to enable another person to do the same, is the key to success in all types of relationship.

MAKING THE MOST
OF YOUR COMBINATION

AS YOU'VE SEEN in chapter four, the interaction of your primary element and your partner's is probably the strongest single factor in overall compatibility. It plays a very strong part in determining how your sexuality, emotions, and basic way of being is likely to interact with your lover's personality; and the traditional Five Element approach rates some combinations a lot more highly than others in terms of conventional workability. However, there are things you can do about this, as you will see, that will improve the worst of situations. Following are some examples to illustrate this. Look at the possibilities for improving the potential of the three different types of element combination.

ABOVE: *The natural law of Yin and Yang.*

COPING WITH
CONFLICTING ELEMENTS

When your Primary Numbers have elements that lie on the control cycle, such as the combination of Metal and Fire or Water and Earth, you're presented with the most challenging basic relationship situation. As described in the previous chapter, there is an inherent opposition of energies and lack of empathy between the elements, in the Primary Number combinations. Obviously, all relationships have their conflicts and their ups and downs, and this is as it should be. It's just that in this case, the ups and downs are going to be a lot more dramatic and extreme, and a more frequent feature between yourself and your partner. The relationship will take longer than others to establish and stabilize, and will be slower to build up trust. In the long run though, the relationship and the way it bonds may be created through facing and surviving difficulties together.

ABOVE: *Find someone who has the primary element most compatible with your own and you'll be off to a good start!*

MAKING A SUCCESS OF A RELATIONSHIP WITH CONFLICTING ELEMENTS

To make a success of such a combination, it is important to create the missing essential relationship dynamics in other ways. This could include:

✳ Keeping channels of communication open
✳ Making a real effort to do things together and often
✳ Going in for activities your lover enjoys, even if they're not your most favorite
✳ Being particularly tolerant of your lover's outlook on life where it differs from your own outlook
✳ Being prepared to compromise in your actions, whilst still preserving your own identity
✳ Trying to really understand what is going on for your lover
✳ Endeavoring to nurture one another
✳ Being sensitive to your partner's needs and sexual preferences
✳ Letting your partner know what you're thinking and feeling, as mind-reading doesn't come easily to you
✳ Keeping in touch when you're apart

All these things may need to be developed and cultivated deliberately, because in this relationship they are that bit less likely to happen as a matter of course.

ABOVE: *Where elements conflict, help your relationship along by keeping in close touch with your partner.*

It will also be important to take account of the direction of control in the Five Element dynamics – to take steps to balance out the natural tendency for one of you to consistently inhibit or constrain the other. For example, Metal will tend to cut back on the freedom of Wood, and Earth will tend to restrict Water. It is therefore important for both of you to take care that one of you doesn't always wield the power, take the initiative, or deprive the other person of their freedom.

USING THE
MEDIATING ELEMENTS

ANOTHER APPROACH that can be taken in this type of relationship is to make up for the energies missing in your combination of opposing elements. Here Feng Shui Astrology has a very cunning trick up its sleeve. If a couple do not share the same element, you have discovered two ways in which their elements can relate to one another:

✳ elements that are on the support cycle
✳ elements that are on the control cycle

However, there is a third cycle of relationship between elements and it can play a key role in the

ABOVE: *If the Water element in a given relationship clashes with the Fire element, then the Wood element can bring a moderating influence.*

improvement of relationship potential. This is known as the Mediating Cycle, illustrated above. As you now know, the elements are traditionally

RIGHT: *If a couple spend more time in their garden, or park, then they become closer to the elements and in particular those that make up their character.*

arranged around the circle in order of supporting relationship, and across the circle in the star-shaped sequence of control. Looking in particular at the control sequence, you can see that each element bypasses the element that is one position round the circle, and controls the one that is next one round in the circular sequence. This bypassed element

FIRE	mediates the conflict between Wood and Earth	
EARTH	mediates the conflict between Fire and Metal	
METAL	mediates the conflict between Earth and Water	
WATER	mediates the conflict between Metal and Wood	
WOOD	mediates the conflict between Water and Fire	

ABOVE: *Table of mediating elements.*

has a special potential for moderating or mitigating the conflict that exists between the elements on either side of it. Thus each element has a mitigating relationship with two others, and the sequence of these creates the Mediating Cycle. The table of mediating combinations is shown above on this page.

So the trick is to bring into your situation the energies of the element that provides this mitigating effect on your conflict of elements. In a combination of Metal and Wood, for instance, you would seek ways of bringing in Water influence – for instance,

LEFT: *The phrase "to commune with nature" has never seemed more true than when seen coupled with Feng Shui Astrology.*

sharing a more fluid approach to life and going with the flow more often. You could even avail yourself of the actual physical presence of water energy, by spending time near it, or having a water feature in your garden or home.

MAKING THE MOST OF SUPPORTING ELEMENTS

IF YOUR PRIMARY elements are connected by the cycle of support, you already have the makings of a more naturally stable and straightforward relationship. Ups and downs will no doubt be there, but they will not be so extreme or abrupt. Nonetheless, pointers can be given to strengthening the potential of the relationship still further, for things can still go wrong. You have a degree of polarity in your combination, but there will not be quite the same dynamic attraction of opposites as in the antagonistic combinations, unless you happen to have attracting numbers. So steps may be taken to enhance excitement and variety in your intimacy and love-making, and in your life together.

There will also be a tendency for the support cycle to have a one-sided effect; one person will tend to be giving most of the supporting, and the other receiving most of it. So it's important to make efforts to share both these roles; avoid building up a situation in which one of you always leads and the other always follows, or where one feels terribly martyred and the other is completely dependent. To avoid this, the person with the supporting element can cultivate the habit of taking the lead more, and the one with the supported element can practice playing a secondary role at times. These role-playing practices should not deny your own basic nature, but rather can be cultivated and applied from time to time.

BELOW: *Like a ship at sea, a relationship can travel through stormy waters as well as calm.*

These relationships are classically regarded as having moderate compatibility – characterized by plenty of familiarity but little "spark." The ups and downs in these relationships may be so few and so small that life can get just a bit too cosy and comfortable, or even dull; you know each other only too well. There is a tendency for each partner to fail to see the other's negative aspects, and even to reinforce these qualities, so that both can descend into a deeper and deeper rut. So, to prevent either one of you being tempted to seek excitement in a more sparky combination somewhere else, it's vital to make the most of whatever polarity does exist in your situation. You can take some common-sense measures – define boundaries within the relationship rather than living in each other's pockets all the time; each of you have a life outside the relationship; take

ABOVE: *Don't let familiarity breed contempt – try surprising your partner!*

separate holidays sometimes, and so on. All these things will increase polarity and therefore attraction and get the "chemistry" working again.

ELEMENTAL INFLUENCES TO INTRODUCE TO SINGLE-ELEMENT COMBINATIONS	
WATER + WATER	Metal, Wood
WOOD + WOOD	Water, Fire
FIRE + FIRE	Wood, Earth
EARTH + EARTH	Fire, Metal
METAL + METAL	Water, Fire

But you also need to go out of your way to introduce the qualities and activities that relate to the other elements – in particular those that are adjacent to yours on the support cycle. Thus, for example, a Water couple could get into the energies of Wood, such as activities that are particularly inspirational. They could also get into the energies of Metal, such as being more forceful, organized, and focused. They need to go beyond their normal ways of being. In love-making and intimacy, they need to create excitement, introduce mystery, and perhaps a touch of danger, so as not to take each other for granted.

In social activities, you can also draw strongly on the energies of particular close friends or family members that you know belong to other elements, for companionship, advice, or influence that can enhance your own situation.

ENHANCING THE
NINE-NUMBER COMBINATIONS

THERE ARE STRATEGIES for maximizing the possibilities of any combination of three numbers, which all essentially involve carrying the above processes a little further. It's always useful to bear in mind while doing this that the matching of Primary Numbers tends to be the most powerful single influence.

In chapter four, you looked at your two sets of numbers and compared them in each of the three personality categories. Now it's time to determine an approach that will help make the most of that potential. For instance, you may have conflicting elements in your Primary Numbers, but your Inner Numbers may be of supporting or identical elements, which greatly eases conflicting energies

ABOVE: *Children can provide the missing element in your combination – although you can't be sure to get the element you want!*

ABOVE: *Supportive Inner Numbers can moderate conflicting Primary Numbers when partners give importance to shared spiritual needs.*

in the relationship. You can give further emphasis to this factor by emphasizing how you relate at this inner or more spiritual level, where your drive or purpose in life resides – connecting and communicating at this level and giving it importance within the relationship. That way, this aspect of your chemistry will play a greater part in the bigger picture. Or perhaps you have, together with the conflicting primary elements, more harmonious elements in your Outer Number category. Although a less powerful influence, it can still be played up by accenting its part in your lives together – valuing your respective outer ways and habits of behavior.

Indeed, relationships where the opposing primary elements are balanced by more compatible dynamics in the other element combinations can form the basis of very workable relationships. The real challenge is where there is a conflict in all three

categories. To get this combination to work for a whole lifetime, you'll probably have to be extremely accommodating, extremely tolerant, and extremely determined to make it work. It can, and will, surely, be done!

You can apply broadly the same principle of behavior where you have identical elements in your Primary Numbers, and more antagonistic element combinations in one of the other categories, by playing up that more polarized aspect of your potential and putting it to some good.

There is, by the way, one other very powerful way of introducing a missing element into your combination – having children! It's a bit of a wild card though, quite apart from coping with the children themselves; the trouble is that you can't really pick your element. You may be able to choose your year; but remember – up to the age of around eighteen years, a child takes its Primary Number from the month of birth, not from the year it was born. Still, it might be worth a try.

Apart from this very radical step there is, however, a further major strategy you can use to get your relationship to work better and the partners involved to flourish. That is to take advantage of how the dynamics of your interaction with each other vary over the course of time – and that is what you shall discover next.

CHAPTER SIX

Your Relationship over Time

Now you know *a great deal about your own astrological make-up as it affects your love-life; you've gained insight into your lover or potential lover's aspects; and you've examined the astrological dynamics of your interaction as a couple. These are all facets of your combined personalities, but time does not stand still. All is subject to changing influences over the passage of time, which is recognized by all astrological systems. First, you personally are subject to differing influences; secondly, your partner is too; and thirdly, so is the combination of your aspects.*

The beauty of Feng Shui Astrology is that the same simple system that gives you information about yourself – the Magic Square – also enables you to plot these important changing influences on your potential destiny. So there's no need to work out complicated charts of the heavens at crucial moments in time. By noting these changing patterns of influence, you will be better able to understand what is going on in any relationship situation; you will be able to maximize your potential as a lover – and the potential of your relationship, whether it is well-established, brand-new, or just about to happen. You can also use this information to understand what you've been experiencing in past relationships. You can use it for the key stages of a relationship – to ascertain the best time to start one, to pop an important question, to settle down, to move in together, or to do some vital reassessment. It can help you to choose the best timing for important decisions and actions.

ABOVE: *Feng Shui Astrology will teach you how to judge the best time for taking decisions and making changes.*

Better still, it enables you to determine which of the two of you will be better placed astrologically to initiate any of these matters, or to play a particular type of role in the relationship, at any time. Examination of the changing houses therefore improves the prospects for success and happiness in all departments of your relationship.

The way in which astrological influences work over time is like this. Every year in the nine-year cycle, as you know, has a different number, and this is what gave you your Primary Number. Each year in the cycle also has a square with a different configuration of numbers, and with the number of that year in the center. These squares are the "maps" by which you can work out the influences on you in any year. But the influences don't just apply to the years; there is also a cycle of nine months, and even a daily cycle too, each with a different level of influence. The yearly cycle has the most profound and far-reaching effects, whilst the daily effects are very fleeting. Working with the daily cycles is rather complex and somewhat beyond the scope of this book.

In this chapter then, you will first of all find out how to work out your position or "house" for any year or month. Then you will discover the classical interpretations of each of these houses – the kind of experience it brings, the strengths and weaknesses, the most likely emotional patterns, the ways in which you are likely to react to a lover or partner, what will work better, and what won't work so well. Lastly, you will be given pointers and strategies for putting all this into practice. Remember, though – none of these houses is "good" or "bad" – only different.

THE NINE HOUSES

WHETHER YOUR'E considering years or months, the Magic Square influences change in a continuously repeating cycle of nine; in each of which one of the numbers is dominant. The dominance of this number in any square is the reason it becomes your number if you are born in that year or that month. This sequence is represented graphically by the set of nine squares which you used in chapter two to discover your third number from the other two. All the other numbers move around to different positions too, as the square changes position in the sequence.

The "standard" square is the one that has 5 in the center, marking the mid-point of the cycle of nine; and it is this square that holds the key to interpreting all the other squares, and the effects of the changes of influence over time. In the standard square, all the numbers are in their "home" places, which represent and summarize all the qualities which you have learned to associate with each number. These home positions, or "houses," are referred to by the numbers that belong there in the standard square. The top left position, for instance, is known as the House of 4 and the bottom middle position is the House of 1.

As time passes, you occupy the houses sequentially, dictating the influences to which you are subject. To ascertain the influences for any month or year, you look at the square that applies to it, and check which position your own Primary Number occupies; you then look to the standard square to see which house this is and then read the corresponding interpretation.

ABOVE: *A good time to move in together? Check the prevailing influences of the Magic Square.*

8	4	6
7	9	2
3	5	1

7	3	5
6	8	1
2	4	9

6	2	4
5	7	9
1	3	8

5	1	3
4	6	8
9	2	7

4	9	2
3	5	7
8	1	6

3	8	1
2	4	6
7	9	5

2	7	9
1	3	5
6	8	4

1	6	8
9	2	4
5	7	3

9	5	7
8	1	3
4	6	2

ABOVE: *Study of the repeating cycle of the nine houses will enable you to plan ahead in all aspects of your relationship.*

Let's put this into practice, using the example couple from the previous chapter. Their primary numbers are:

PERSON A – 8

PERSON B – 7

BIRTHDATE	PRIMARY NUMBER		
	1 OR 4 OR 7	2 OR 5 OR 8	3 OR 6 OR 9
FEBRUARY 4 TO MARCH 5	**8**	**2**	**5**
MARCH 6 TO APRIL 4	**7**	**1**	**4**
APRIL 5 TO MAY 5	**6**	**9**	**3**
MAY 6 TO JUNE 5	**5**	**8**	**2**
JUNE 6 TO JULY 7	**4**	**7**	**1**
JULY 8 TO AUGUST 7	**3**	**6**	**9**
AUGUST 8 TO SEPTEMBER 7	**2**	**5**	**8**
SEPTEMBER 8 TO OCTOBER 8	**1**	**4**	**7**
OCTOBER 9 TO NOVEMBER 7	**9**	**3**	**6**
NOVEMBER 8 TO DECEMBER 7	**8**	**2**	**5**
DECEMBER 8 TO JANUARY 5	**7**	**1**	**4**
JANUARY 6 TO FEBRUARY 3	**6**	**9**	**3**

ABOVE: *By maximizing your potential as you pass through each different house, you are working closely with the cosmic energies.*

Whether considering a year or month situation, Person A will always be looking for the position occupied by the number 8. In a year or month governed by the number 1, for instance – the square with 1 at the center – this will be the left middle position, which on the standard square is the House of 3. Person A will therefore be experiencing the influence of the number 3 in that particular period.

In that same period of time, Person B will be in the House of 2, because number 7 occupies the top right position, which represents the number 2 position in the standard square.

Therefore, all you need to know now, in order to discover your house occupancy in any year or month, is which square applies to it – that is, which number is at the center; in other words, which is the number of that year or month. This is exactly the same information you used in chapter two to find out your first two numbers. These steps are summarized here. Squares for current years and months are also shown to save you the trouble.

CALCULATING THE YEAR NUMBER

The number for any year can be calculated with the formula below.

✳ Add together the four digits of the year

✳ If this new number is greater than ten, add its two digits together to produce a single-figure number

✳ Subtract this number from 11, and you get the year number

For example, the year 2001:

$$2001 = 2 + 0 + 0 + 1 = 3$$

$$11 - 3 = 8$$

So 2001 is an 8 year; its square is the one with 8 at the center.

Remember, as before, that the Chinese year begins on February 4, not January 1!

The square for any month is the one with that month's number at the center, which is derived from the monthly table; remember here that the months do not start on the first calendar day.

CALCULATING THE PAST AND FUTURE

The squares for the years 1999 to 2007 are shown on this page. You can easily work backward or forward from this set, for the center numbers simply change from 1 to 9 repeatedly.

The sample squares for the months December 1998 to May 2000 are shown opposite. You can carry on this series backward or forward, as the numbers at the center again change from 1 to 9

RIGHT: Anyone can learn to interpret the Magic Square and lead a more fulfilling and effective life.

1999

9	5	7
8	1	3
4	6	2

2000

8	4	6
7	9	2
3	5	1

2001

7	3	5
6	8	1
2	4	9

2002

6	2	4
5	7	9
1	3	8

2003

5	1	3
4	6	8
9	2	7

2004

4	9	2
3	5	7
8	1	6

2005

3	8	1
2	4	6
7	9	5

2006

2	7	9
1	3	5
6	8	4

2007/1998

1	6	8
9	2	4
5	7	3

repeatedly; or calculate them from the monthly table. Remember: the months do not start on their first calendar day; if in doubt, check against the table.

ABOVE: *You will learn how to pick the right moment for that important meeting or relationship decision.*

Create your own blank squares on these models, so that you can mark in the numbers and label the squares for a set of years or months in which you are particularly interested.

Now you have the knowledge to work out the house you will occupy – or did occupy – in any month or year, in the past or future. So what do all these houses mean?

LEFT: *You can plan the perfect moment for taking your friendship one step further!*

THE SQUARES FOR DECEMBER 1998–MAY 2000

DEC. 1998

9	5	7
8	1	3
4	6	2

JAN. 1999

8	4	6
7	9	2
3	5	1

FEB. 1999

7	3	5
6	8	1
2	4	9

MAR. 1999

6	2	4
5	7	9
1	3	8

APR. 1999

5	1	3
4	6	8
9	2	7

MAY 1999

4	9	2
3	5	7
8	1	6

JUNE 1999

3	8	1
2	4	6
7	9	5

JULY 1999

2	7	9
1	3	5
6	8	4

AUG. 1999

1	6	8
9	2	4
5	7	3

SEP. 1999

9	5	7
8	1	3
4	6	2

OCT. 1999

8	4	6
7	9	2
3	5	1

NOV. 1999

7	3	5
6	8	1
2	4	9

DEC. 1999

6	2	4
5	7	9
1	3	8

JAN. 2000

5	1	3
4	6	8
9	2	7

FEB. 2000

4	9	2
3	5	7
8	1	6

MAR. 2000

3	8	1
2	4	6
7	9	5

APR. 2000

2	7	9
1	3	5
6	8	4

MAY 2000

1	6	8
9	2	4
5	7	3

EXPLORING THE NINE ASTROLOGICAL HOUSES

There is a close relationship between the experience of occupying any house and the characteristics of the personality that goes with that number; for it is the astrological influence of that house which formed those characteristics. It's as if you explore your potential to become that type of person for a while, as you pass through their house, even though you yourself are fundamentally another type of person. Let's now look at the generic characteristics of the nine houses. These will clearly require interpretation of scale, according to whether you are doing a yearly or monthly analysis. You will also see there is a very strong underlying pattern of sequence of the houses, analogous to the cycle of the natural world and the seasons. As you pass successively through the nine stages, there is a sense of progressive development, like the progress from a seed, represented by the number 1 house, to full maturity and blossoming, signified by the House of 9. In terms of Yin and Yang, there is a sense of upward growth, or rising and

BELOW: *Preparing the soil according to the natural cycle. We can apply this analogy to making preparations in our own life.*

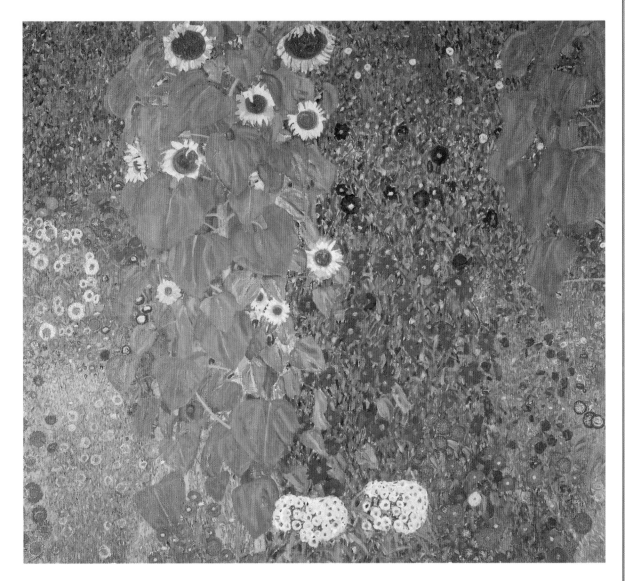

ABOVE: *In the House of 9 the upward Yin energies have reached their peak. This is a time of maximum energy and activity.*

expanding energies, in the first half of the cycle, from 1 to 4; and a feeling of more inward or gathering energy in the second half, from 5 to 8. Hence, making the most of your true potential in each different house not only benefits you at the time; it also builds on the progress of earlier stages, and contributes to the success of the future. If you take these influences into account, you will be working with the energies of the cosmos, the universe, and the planet, rather than against them. In this way, everything you do can be a lot more effective.

THE HOUSE OF 1
MOVING WATER
DARKNESS

THIS HOUSE corresponds to the dormancy of midwinter, when there can be a feeling of "descent into the underworld"; but it is an excellent time to reflect on the past, make plans for the future, and focus on inner personal development, rather than more tangible outward or social progress. Difficulty is likely to be experienced from trying to achieve too much in the tangible sense; it isn't a good time for starting new projects and taking new directions, but rather for making the inner preparations that will help these succeed in future houses. It's best to let events take their course and go with the flow of life's river. In classical Chinese parlance, this is the time for the yielding or non-striving state of Taoism. Your intuition, though, can be extremely strong and reliable at this time, so it's good to cultivate your ability to tune into it.

ABOVE: *The symbol of Moving Water urges us to go with the flow.*

In love and relationship, difficulty may be experienced, often caused by others rather than yourself, due to the passive characteristics of this house. Your intentions can easily be misunderstood, and arguments and conflicts you get into will probably be lost. The most common of the painful

ABOVE: *Trees rest and gather strength in the House of 1 stage.*

NUMBER ONE

The House of 1 is a house of relection and intuition and so you should:

* master your passiveness
* use your intuition wisely
* not be afraid to go with the flow
* avoid negative vibes

emotions you are likely to encounter is fearfulness. As you can be vulnerable at this time, try to avoid the influence of those who are negatively inclined.

THE HOUSE OF 2
THE EARTH
RECEPTIVITY

THIS POSITION continues the quality of slowness in outward progress that began in the House of 1, but the outlook begins to brighten. The ground of your life is becoming ready for new growth, but that growth is not as yet outwardly evident. It continues to be a good time for self-development and also for strengthening

ABOVE: *A time of special sensitivity to the needs of others.*

it is inherently a passing phase. The fluctuating emotions can also have an upsetting effect on those close to you; if so, it can be helpful to rein them in a bit. On the positive side, this is when you will have greater than usual potential for nurturing those around you.

ABOVE: *Yin energies are strong in the House of 2. This is a good time to start that new project*

friendships. It is ideal for "cleaning up your act" in preparation for occupation of the following houses and the opportunity they will bring.

There can still tend to be uncertainty in love and romance. And there may be a tendency to worry or be anxious; but try not to over-react to this, as

NUMBER TWO

The House of 2 is a house of self-development, and so you should:

* take advantage and develop friendships
* put your mind to self-improvement
* try not to be anxious in love and romance
* stay within your own limitations

THE HOUSE OF 3
THUNDER
PROCEEDING

THIS POSITION represents the first, strong, tangible growth and forward movement of spring; everything seems a lot brighter and your energies are more strongly active. It's a terrific time to start anything going and for advancing toward your goals and ambitions. At this time it's appropriate to act quickly, seize opportunities, and proceed steadily and energetically.

RIGHT: *Teenagers can be impatient and argumentative at this time!*

ABOVE: *The sound of Thunder signals approaching activity in the House of 3.*

At the same time, these strong energies may have a down side. Difficult emotions that can surface in this house most strongly are impatience, frustration, or anger, particularly if you come up against people or things that seem to block your progress. This energy is classically represented by what happens to you at sixteen years old, when you are always in this house – the age when in many cultures you can start having legal sex!

NUMBER THREE

The House of 3 is a house of forward movement and growth, and so you should:

✳ act quickly and seize opportunities

✳ proceed energetically but steadily

✳ not become impatient or frustrated

Love and romance are more actively mobile in your life in this house, whether for the year or month; a new relationship might start, or an existing one be renewed. It's a good time to take the lead in exploring new activities with a partner and making new variations on your old patterns. If things have become stuck between you, this is the perfect time to shift everything forward. But remember that your lover may not be feeling quite so dynamic; so take this into account in your plans, and take care to appreciate him or her fully – which might not be what comes naturally at this time.

THE HOUSE OF 4
WIND
PREPARATION

THIS IS WHERE the earlier, dramatic first energies of earlier spring now disperse and lose their quality of single, unstoppable direction, becoming the more diffuse energy of later spring. The outlook is still bright, but the forward progress initiated in the previous house goes into a deeper level of development. Continuing with these processes will generally be more fruitful than starting off brand-new activities and ventures, or starting out in completely new directions.

ABOVE: *The powerful spring energies start to disperse in the House of 4. Take care not to be blown off course.*

NUMBER FOUR

The House of 4 is a house of deeper, slower development, a transitional stage with energies dissipating, and so you should:

✴ remember discipline is the key in this house
✴ avoid anything hasty or impulsive
✴ keep an open mind

The quality of dispersal of energies also makes itself felt like a wind that can blow in all directions – strongly or softly. So it's helpful to have a plan for everything important that you do, in order to keep up the forward momentum and avoid dissipating beneficial forces. It is particularly important to avoid being hasty or impulsive. As with the previous house, also of the element Wood, you may find yourself responding to hindrance with frustration, impatience, or anger in extreme cases.

Relationships that have already begun can benefit greatly at this time, continuing to develop and grow, with increasing trust and harmony. At the same time, you'll need to keep an open mind, take special care to be aware of your partner's needs, and be wary of the high emotional ideals that you may be harboring.

This house marks the end of the Yin, upward energy cycle, settling into the House of 5.

THE HOUSE OF 5
THE CENTER
FLUCTUATION

THIS POSITION is the ultimate point of balance – between Yin and Yang forces, between the upward-growing and the inward-settling energies, between the poles of heaven and earth. It has the quality of being at the center of things, where everything tends to move toward you without your shifting. This includes the products of all these extremes, both positive and negative.

陰陽

ABOVE: *At the transition point of the House of 5, Yin and Yang are balanced.*

In the sequence of the nine houses, it is the point of transition from upward growth to inward consolidation. It is a time of gathering. Being a pivotal time, actions taken from this position have more power invested in them, and therefore greater effect, for better or for worse. There are likely to be bigger ups and downs for you in this house – but at the same time you will probably find yourself better equipped than usual to deal with them.

It is a time to take care, to be cautious, to rely on your potential for stability, to stay within the limits of your ability, and in your journey through this house be open to input and advice from others. You'll find yourself wanting to be the center of attention and of other people's activities, but try not to let this get out of hand. Whatever flexibility you can muster will help a great deal.

This is, in fact, the house you were born into, because in the square of your birth year your number always occupies the central position. You enter this house again after two nine-year cycles, when you are eighteen – another pivotal time, poised between childhood and adulthood.

In love and romance, too, you may be exposed to extremes of positive and negative, including things you thought belonged strictly to the past. Your partner may also experience these strong effects through you and your powerful influence on others when in this house; he or she may begin to perceive you as split into two quite different personalities or ways of being. So take care to talk things through with him or her and to listen carefully to what he or she has to say.

BELOW: *Like a tranquil fall landscape, the House of 5 is a place of balance.*

ABOVE: *The House of 5 is the house you were born into.*

NUMBER FIVE

5

The House of 5 is a point of balance and transition, and so you should:

✴ take care and be cautious
✴ rely on your potential for stability
✴ stay within your own limitations
✴ be open to the advice of others
✴ remain flexible
✴ not let your desire to be at the center get out of hand

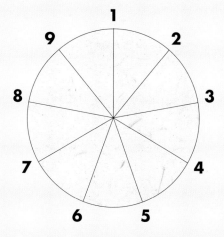

ABOVE: *The House of 5 is the resting point of the nine-year cycle.*

THE HOUSE OF 6

HEAVEN
PROSPERITY

THIS POSITION relates to the time of early fall and to the harvest – the reaping of benefits from efforts put into the previous five stages. It is a house in which enterprises can more easily bring their rewards, and is traditionally regarded as a materially favorable and fortunate house for those passing through it.

ABOVE: *Our goal and reward are in sight in the House of 6.*

It is also a good time to enjoy life, to celebrate, and to follow desires. On the other hand, it's important to guard against overconfidence or arrogance, and it will be wise to listen to the advice of others. Likewise, the fruits of success – whether physical, material, emotional, sexual, or whatever – need to be managed appropriately and not squandered, akin to the grain from the harvest that has to be stored and measured out, to last through to the next fall.

NUMBER SIX

The House of 6 is a house of reward and fruition, and so you should:

* enjoy life and follow your desires
* reap the rewards of past planning
* take time to improve your own resources

This is a time when you can deepen your own personal resources – your wisdom and maturity, your sense of responsibility, and capacity to meet life's demands when less fortunate times come later. You will have been occupying this house, for instance, when you reached nineteen years, in many cultures the age for leaving school to go out into the world or graduate to higher education.

Similarly, your romance and relationship can gain strength, deepen, and stabilize. Your partner may instinctively recognize the strength and authority of your position, and support you in the steps that you take to improve the status quo. Yet it's worth saying again – beware of thinking you always know what's best for everyone else.

THE HOUSE OF 7
THE LAKE
JOY

THIS IS THE SECOND phase of fall qualities, when energies settle still further. There is celebration now that the harvest is gathered in and earlier efforts continue to bear fruit; life has a quality of smoothness and ease. A more mellow type of satisfaction and happiness now evolves – materially, mentally, and emotionally.

ABOVE: *Now you can relax a little and enjoy the results of all your endeavors.*

What pays off best, therefore, is to be fairly conservative – stick to what you know, rather than stepping out into the unfamiliar. As the saying goes, "If it ain't broke, don't fix it!" Your inner maturity can continue to develop here, with the benefit of self-reflection, and often with a spiritual dimension or the gaining of insight about life. There is also the ability to inspire others. This house is entered, for instance, at the common retirement age of 65.

In terms of intimate relationship, there is a stronger than usual attraction to the opposite sex, but new encounters at this time are not likely to be profound or long-lasting. Affairs here are likely to produce unhappiness all round. Also watch out for a tendency to jealousy. When things aren't going so well, the emotions you are likely to feel most strongly may be sadness or depression. Take care not to become too isolated; communication within your relationship is particularly important.

THE HOUSE OF 8
THE MOUNTAIN
STILLNESS

THIS IS A TIME OF accumulation of energies into the stillness of the mountain, which also offers the prospect of far-sighted perspective. It is a time of the turning of energies, too, before the dramatic spectacle of being in the House of 9. Often associated with revolution, it is a time when many things in your life can change, including your way of thinking. The classic turning-point years of twenty-one and thirty belong to this house.

Correspondingly, it's an excellent opportunity to review yourself and your whole situation, and consider what bits are worth keeping and what should be let go. With the capacity for far-sighted vision, it is also wise to beware of egocentricity, aloofness, stubbornness, or fixed points of view.

Romantically, this can be a great time to clear up outstanding items on the agenda that are left over from the past and that may be causing frustration.

ABOVE: *A desire for change can turn into revolution in the House of 8.*

NUMBER EIGHT

The House of 8 is a house given to change and far-sighted thought, and so you should:

* re-evaluate who you are and where you are going
* avoid stubbornness and aloofness
* aid romance by clearing up outstanding troubles

ABOVE: *Taking the wider view. This is an excellent time for reviewing your life.*

This can greatly brighten the future. Your partner may well have difficulty knowing what's going on with your emotions, for you may be more vulnerable, yet less revealing, than usual. So make sure to express clearly what's going on for you and what you want from the relationship. Jealousy or guilt could rear their ugly heads.

THE HOUSE OF 9

FIRE
BRIGHTNESS

THIS IS THE TIME OF full maturity, illumination, and clarity, when the nine-house cycle reaches its peak of fulfillment, like the bright blossoming forth of flowers in the summer. It is an extremely active time, when you'll find you're able to do most of what you want to do. You will have lots of new ideas, and the opportunity to realize long-held dreams or ambitions – especially if you've taken the opportunities provided by the other houses to do the groundwork. However, it's wise

NUMBER NINE

The House of 9 is the house that completes the cycle. It is an extremely active time, one of illumination and clarity, and so you should:

✳ realize long-held dreams
✳ take advantage of flourishing loves
✳ fulfill your ambitions

ABOVE: *Now is the time to go for it – and fulfill those personal ambitions.*

at this time to be wary of extremes, and to be orderly and organized in your way of going about life, in order to minimize the chaotic potential you may have in this house.

Relations with others can be very positive. Love and romance can flourish; encounters may be plentiful but not necessarily deep. You can make many new friends, but may lose old ones. In any existing long-term relationship, it could be good to guard against your whirlwind emotions having too disturbing an effect on your partner.

It may also be difficult for anyone close to you to keep up with the high levels of your energy and personal evolution, which can prove frustrating for you and upsetting for them. Be aware, too, that others around you may be more grounded than you and take advantage of this.

Lots of things about you may well become known now, for this is a period of revelation. Some of these home truths may not please you, but if you've been covering something up, it may be better to come clean now than be found out!

INTERPRETATION
OF YOUR HOUSES

WHILST THESE ARE the overall characteristics of the different houses, there are a number of factors to bear in mind when considering your own fortunes. These include how to apply the information in different ways to years and to months; the varying effects of the houses on people of different numbers and elements; and how to make the most of the two houses that you and your partner occupy at any time.

YOUR YEAR AND MONTH HOUSES

The effect of being in any house is clearly more deep-seated and long-lasting for a year than for a month, and is interpreted accordingly. Also, as the house you occupy in any year is one stage of a nine-year cycle, the potential for what you can achieve and what you will experience in that year will have repercussions throughout the whole of the nine-year period. Correspondingly, your experience and actions whilst occupying any house for any month has an effect throughout a nine-month period – the gestation period, as it happens, for human beings.

ABOVE: *The Chinese character for division and disease.*

So the monthly interpretation is about more immediate and short-term effects, and applies more to transient aspects of your being, especially emotions, than to the broad shifts in the pattern of your life; the realm of the yearly pattern.

ABOVE: *Each nine-month cycle is affected by your actions and reactions in each of the nine houses.*

It's also important to realize that, as both cycles are being experienced at the same time, the web of monthly effects is superimposed onto the year pattern. So in a year of being in the House of 9, let's say, you'll also be passing through twelve phases that include all the monthly houses. Now, some of these superimpositions will reinforce each other – most obviously, when you're also in the monthly House of 9 – while others will have a more neutralizing effect; such as when you're in the House of 1 for the month. There are a range of other combination effects, too, which will become clear as we look at the ways in which different numbers react in different houses.

So in practice, every single month in the whole nine-year cycle is a quite unique combination of year and month influences, enabling you to weave an incredibly rich and varied tapestry from the fabric of your life and the relationships that prove its thread. You will now see there's absolutely no excuse for complaining that "…things never seem to change!" If you're feeling this way, you're not taking advantage of your life's infinitely varied potential. You are limiting yourself.

ABOVE: *You can make the most of every phase of the year by recognizing the potential of each house you occupy.*

with others. Both of these are mainly to do with the interaction of your native element and the element of the house occupied. Generally speaking, when you are in a house of similar or supporting element, you will feel more comfortable and at home. When you are in a house of counteracting element, you will tend to feel a little bit "out of your element" and generally need to be a bit more careful about what you do. A table of the numbers, together with their counteracting numbers, is given below.

EFFECTS OF THE HOUSE ON YOUR NUMBER

These effects fall into two categories – those which affect you and those which affect your interaction

YOUR NUMBER	COUNTERACTING NUMBERS
1	2 5 8 9
2 5 8	1 3 4
3 4	2 5 6 7 8
6 7	3 4 9
9	1 6 7

You will also tend to have somewhat differing dynamics of relationship with other people, according to what house you are currently occupying. In keeping with the way the elements and numbers work, you may feel differing effects. When you are in House of 9, for instance, people whose primary number is 9 will seem somehow familiar

LEFT: *Your affinity with others will vary according to the different houses you are occupying at the time.*

and more understandable. They will seem to be your natural allies, supporters, or advisers, for they are permanently in tune with what you are temporarily going through. People with antagonistic elements to that of your house, however, will interact with you quite differently. A number 1 person, for instance, may seem to be your opponent, because they are ruled by Water, whilst a 6 or 7 person, being Metal, might have that impression about you. But none of this runs very deep; it's more a question of temporary reactions and can easily be overcome by reflection and clear communication.

In terms of love and romance, the phenomenon of attracting numbers may make a more dramatic impact through your house position, especially for the year. You may notice you are particularly attracted to people whose Primary Number occupies the opposite position in the Magic Square to yours. So when you're in that House of 9, you may find yourself drawn to number 1 people – even though their energies are elementally opposed to what you are currently experiencing. The following year, when you are in House of 1, you might suddenly be noticing only 9 people! If so, it will be good to bear in mind that this too is a transitory attraction, and is not nearly as strong a basis for making a long-term relationship as one based on

NUMBER	ATTRACTING NUMBER
1	9
2	8
3	7
4	6
5	5
6	4
7	3
8	2
9	1

LEFT: *Share roles with your partner, taking on whichever tasks are best suited to the houses you are occupying at the time.*

your birth chart and theirs. Of course, you might just want a quick fling; something short-lived.

If you're already in an ongoing partnership, there is another way in which this dynamic appears. You and your lover will feel particularly strong romantic and sexual attraction when the two of you happen to be occupying these opposite houses. These sets of attracting house numbers are summarized left. In fact, the pattern of your whole relationship will be somewhat affected by the interaction of the pairs of houses you are respectively occupying at any time, in line with the now-familiar principles of the interaction of elements and numbers.

ROLE-SHARING AND INITIATIVE

One of the most powerful ways for you as a couple to make creative use of this information is to exploit the characteristics of the houses you respectively occupy at any time. Let whichever of you is in a more favorable position for certain roles, responsibilities, or activities be in charge of those, on behalf of you both. So, for instance, the person who is occupying the number 6 house can naturally do more of the decision-making and organize any celebrations, whilst a partner who is in the number 2 house can focus on advance preparation for something in the future, such as moving home or taking a holiday.

SYNCHRONIZE YOUR HOUSES: PAST AND PRESENT

You can also maximize your joint potential by working constructively with the interaction of the elements of the houses you occupy. When the elements of your houses are the same, you can get to know each other a lot better. When these elements are in supporting connection, such as Fire and Earth, you can build up the relationship's storehouse of harmony and mutual understanding. In this situation, it will be advantageous for you both if the person in the supported position, in this case Earth, takes more initiative in joint matters, and the person in the supporting position – Fire – does more of the backing up. When the houses you occupy have antagonistic elements, you may find it helpful to counteract any difficulties by staying in touch,

RIGHT: The House of 6 is a good time to plan those special celebrations.

ABOVE: *The houses occupied by you and your partner will have far-reaching effects on major events in your lives.*

working on communication, and keeping differences of opinion or conflict in perspective. At the same time, you may also have the opportunity to enjoy the increased interest or attraction that can come from the added polarity and differences. Again, the person in the controlling position can take more initiative than the other, whose actions will tend to be dampened. All these dynamics will naturally have a greater impact in the houses of the years than the houses of the months; and of course, the month pattern will be going on over the background pattern of the years.

It can be extremely illuminating to look back over key times in your life and see what houses you were occupying at the time, whether for yourself or for your lover, or to compare the dynamics of both of these together.

CHAPTER SEVEN

Taking it Further

You're now in *possession of an incredibly powerful tool for increasing your happiness, fulfillment, and success in matters of love, sex, and relationships. You now know how to draw on more of your own personal resources, how to choose a partner or lover more appropriately, how to make the very best of an ongoing relationship, and how to deal creatively with the way your relationship is changing over time. Let's now look at some guidelines for making even more use of the information which is now at your fingertips.*

OTHER TYPES OF RELATIONSHIP

The principles covered in this book can be applied not only to the dynamics of intimate liaisons, but also to other close relationships. These combinations of personalities depend on much the same factors, and raise much the same questions. What are the classic ingredients for a harmonious partnership? What causes antagonism, strife, and difficulty in achieving the partnership's goals? What strategies can be employed to get the very best out of any given kind of partnership? These questions can be answered in exactly the same way as for lovers; sex may not come into it, but the astrological influences apply in exactly parallel ways.

You could apply your new-found insights, for example, to close family relationships; and

LEFT: *Feng Shui Astrology can be applied to other important relationships, such as business partnerships.*

ABOVE: *Understanding the elements of support and control in those people close to you can lead to increased harmony.*

this could help you fathom what's been going on for all these years. It could also assist in getting things to work better in the future in areas where there has been difficulty in the past. In business, these principles could be the means of wisely choosing a new partner, thus increasing the chances of prosperity and avoiding a potentially disastrous experience. A business partnership, after all, is often compared with a marriage – except that it can be harder to get out of and even costlier if it goes wrong! Other situations you might look at could include your relationship with a close bosom pal, people with whom you share your home, or close working arrangements.

Whatever the situation, the principles work in just the same ways. With your family, for example, you may for the first time come to understand why you've so long felt suppressed by your mother, validated by your father, and experienced bitter rivalry with your sister Could it be something to do with your mother's element controlling yours, your father's element supporting yours, and your sister having antagonistic elements in three personality categories? With this information you'll probably be able to relate a whole lot better to your own offspring; family life should then be improved, if that's what's happening in your life.

LEFT: *Astrology can show you how and when to find the perfect partnership – but you still have to work at it!*

Seeking that business partner, you might suddenly realize, just in time, that you really should reject the overtures from that very enthusiastic and charismatic gentleman, because his numbers are completely incompatible with yours. Instead, you can hold out for someone who has sufficient differences from you to make a good combination of skills between you, but enough harmony as well; someone with whom you have an identical Inner Number would be ideal.

It may become clear to you, too, why there was a little boy that you were inseparable from at school and another that you made life hell for – and now that situation is completely reversed, when you are all adults. It has dawned on you that your respective childhood numbers all worked one way and your adult numbers all the other way. Suddenly, it all makes perfect sense.

Your chosen room-mate or lodger can now be someone that eventually becomes a life-long friend, rather than someone else who steals your ice-cream in the middle of the night and can never own up to you about it, because your numbers provide for no communication whatsoever. At work, using the principles of Feng Shui Astrology could make the creation of a close-knit, harmonious project team a whole lot easier.

POINTERS FOR SUCCESS

The information in this book is only part of a rich and fascinating wider subject that applies to all facets of life, as well as relationships. But if you apply everything in these pages, you can radically improve your love life and personal happiness.

ABOVE: *With different combinations of numbers, the kid you hated at school could become a great friend in adult life.*

Yet the astrological aspect is still only half of any situation; the other factor is what you do about the situation once you've obtained your insights.

No relationship will run smoothly on favorable astrological factors alone; no matter how much you know about the machinery of your relationship – no matter how good your "owner's manual" is – you still have to actually get the thing to work. So it all still comes down to the same familiar ingredients for relationship success – old chestnuts like commitment, respect, trust, give-and-take, and all the rest of them. The difference is that the astrology can help you solve the age-old mystery of which of them to focus on – and when!

The best overall approach to applying this theory is discerning the underlying principles of this system of astrology – the nature of the influencing energies – rather than using the information from the tables and diagrams inflexibly and without understanding. This way, you will get a more profound grasp of the system; you will gain deeper insights; you will be able to adapt the principles to the kaleidoscopic variety of individuals and situations that exist; you will be able to work out the answers when something doesn't quite seem to follow the predicted pattern. Remember, the indications provided here are, by their nature, overall tendencies and underlying patterns, rather than fixed rules giving fixed results; when they operate in life, there are always all kinds of other factors playing their part in the situation.

ABOVE: *Understanding all the types of influence will give you an ongoing insight into your own and others' lives and emotions.*

We are all unique – all six billion-odd of us living on this planet.

If you become familiar with all the types of influence and not just the ones that feature in your chart, this will also pay off; for not only will you understand the people around you better, but you will also have a much deeper grasp of the nature of the nine houses through which you are perpetually passing and which are so closely related to the nine types of personality energies.

Remember, also, that life never stands still. You can derive understanding into how you are in general, and how a situation is now, but the forces acting upon you are never static – this is the integral message

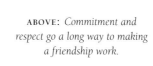

ABOVE: *Commitment and respect go a long way to making a friendship work.*

of Feng Shui Astrology. So ongoing reappraisal is necessary, not only to know what is happening, but to adapt and harmonize with it in order to live life to the best of your ability. Standing still means losing out.

WHAT FENG SHUI ASTROLOGY GIVES YOU

Feng Shui Astrology ensures that you can:

* Live life to the fullest and best of your ability, using your creativity, instinct, judgement, and free will
* Develop as a person and grow positively in your wisdom
* Come to understand others more fully and strengthen your relationships
* Understand life's energies and the kinds of people around you
* Learn that nothing is predictable

More important still, nothing is absolutely predetermined. It's a mistake to think that the indications or predictions from any astrological system – ancient or modern, Eastern or Western, however sophisticated or highly developed – are carved in stone. We always interact with the energies, using our creativity, instinct, judgement, and free will. Nevertheless, you can probably only manifest your greatest potential if you also take into account the forces and natural laws of the universe around you. Feng Shui Astrology, this ageless and extraordinary Oriental system of knowledge and philosophy, is one of the finest ways to tune into these cosmic patterns.

TAPPING IN TO THE UNIVERSE

As you become more experienced and more familiar with how the whole subtle and intricate pattern of energies and influences works, you will find that applying it can become second nature to you. You will notice yourself guessing people's numbers without discovering their birth data; or you know you're in a certain astrological house, without

ABOVE: *Life means constant change and we have to be prepared to adapt and move on with it.*

ABOVE: With practice, we can all learn to tune into the natural energies and live intuitively, in accordance with ourselves.

checking. This is when it gets really interesting, really rewarding, and really effective; for you've now entered the intuitive phase. You're starting to tune into the energies and pick up on them with the subtle sensitivities we all have as human beings; bypassing the conscious mind. With time and practice, this can be a more powerful resource than the conscious mental faculty, which is all too often clouded by emotion, prejudice, or the wish to believe that what you hope for is true. If you succeed in developing this profound, intuitive connection with the material, you will discover all the more about your own truest nature, and realize all the more of your highest potential. You will truly be in rhythm with life and your true self.

So please use this amazing oracle to reach out for whatever you want in your precious connection to other beings: more freedom and less control, perhaps; more ecstasy and less agony; more mystery, fun, excitement, intimacy, closeness, passion, companionship, and eroticism. More love. Go for it!

DIY MAGIC SQUARES

CHAPTER SIX SHOWED YOU how to work out the Magic Square that applies to any year or month, and showed the squares for upcoming periods. But you may want to have the squares in front of you for years or months ahead of these as time passes, or to refer back to particular times in the past. If so you can use the squares on these pages, by simply labeling these with a sequence of year or month dates. Once you have calculated the central number for any year or month, the rest of the squares will follow sequentially. You can then use the squares as shown in chapter six, to find out which house you or your lover occupy at any point in time – past, present, or future. Remember, as before, that the Oriental year starts in February and that the month starts later too.

YEAR SQUARES

9 5 7	8 4 6	7 3 5
8 1 3	7 9 2	6 8 1
4 6 2	3 5 1	2 4 9

6 2 4	5 1 3	4 9 2
5 7 9	4 6 8	3 5 7
1 3 8	9 2 7	8 1 6

3 8 1	2 7 9	1 6 8
2 4 6	1 3 5	9 2 4
7 9 5	6 8 4	5 7 3

9 5 7	8 4 6	7 3 5	9 5 7	8 4 6	7 3 5
8 1 3	7 9 2	6 8 1	8 1 3	7 9 2	6 8 1
4 6 2	3 5 1	2 4 9	4 6 2	3 5 1	2 4 9

6 2 4	5 1 3	4 9 2	6 2 4	5 1 3	4 9 2
5 7 9	4 6 8	3 5 7	5 7 9	4 6 8	3 5 7
1 3 8	9 2 7	8 1 6	1 3 8	9 2 7	8 1 6

3 8 1	2 7 9	1 6 8	3 8 1	2 7 9	1 6 8
2 4 6	1 3 5	9 2 4	2 4 6	1 3 5	9 2 4
7 9 5	6 8 4	5 7 3	7 9 5	6 8 4	5 7 3

9 5 7	8 4 6	7 3 5
8 1 3	7 9 2	6 8 1
4 6 2	3 5 1	2 4 9

6 2 4	5 1 3	4 9 2
5 7 9	4 6 8	3 5 7
1 3 8	9 2 7	8 1 6

3 8 1	2 7 9	1 6 8
2 4 6	1 3 5	9 2 4
7 9 5	6 8 4	5 7 3

INDEX

PICTURE CREDITS

REFERENCES

Nine Star Ki Michio Kushi
(One Peaceful World Press, Becket, Massachusetts, 1995)
Feng Shui Astrology Jan Sandifer (Piatkus, 1997)
An Anthology of I Ching WA Sherill and WK Chu (Arkana, 1989)
The Ki Takashi Yoshikawa (St Martin's Press, 1986)
The Nine Ki Handbook S Gagne and J Mann
(Spiralbound Books, Rochester, NY, 1985)
The I Ching Richard Wilhelm (Routledge & Kegan Paul, 1951)
Gerry Thompson can be contacted at
42 Stanford Road, Brighton, BN1 5DJ, U.K.
Tel: +44(0) 1273 206000